The Collected Essays of Virginia Woolf

by

Virginia Woolf

British Library Cataloguing-in-Publication Data
A catalogue record for this book is available from the
British Library

Contents

Virginia Woolf

Virginia Woolf was born Adeline Virginia Stephen in Kensington, London, England in 1882. Her father, Leslie Stephen, was a respected man of letters, and as a young girl Woolf was introduced to many literary figures, including Henry James. Woolf also made great use of the family home's vast library, working her way through much of the English literary canon as a teenager. Her summers were spent in St. Ives, Cornwall, which would later form the setting for her famous novel, To the Lighthouse.

In 1895, when Woolf was just thirteen, her mother died, triggering the first of her many mental breakdowns. Despite this, between 1897 and 1901 she was able to take courses in Greek, Latin, German and history at the Ladies' Department of King's College London. She even began publishing work with the Times Literary Supplement. However, in 1904, following the death of her father, Woolf suffered another breakdown which saw her briefly institutionalised.

Following her discharge, Woolf and her sisters moved from their family home to a new abode in Bloomsbury. It was here that Woolf met Lytton Strachey, John Maynard Keynes, E. M. Forster and various other writers and intellectuals, who together would form the famous Bloomsbury Set. In 1912, Woolf married author Leonard Woolf, who nursed her through another breakdown and suicide attempt. Woolf published her first novel, The Voyage Out, in 1915. This, as well as various essays, quickly established her as a major public intellectual.

During the twenties, Woolf published the novels that established her as a leading figure of modernism and one of the greatest British novelists of the 20th century: Jacob's Room (1922), Mrs. Dalloway (1925), To the Lighthouse (1927) and Orlando (1928). Stylistically, Woolf experimented with a lyrical stream-of-consciousness narrative mode, and is now considered – along with fellow modernist James Joyce – one of the finest innovators in the English language. Her work has been translated into fifty languages, and her major novels have never been out of print.

After completing her last novel, Between the Acts, Woolf fell into a period of deep depression – exacerbated by the the onset of World War II and the destruction of her home during the Blitz. In 1941, fearing a total mental collapse, Woolf committed suicide. She was 59 years old.

THE COMMON READER

There is a sentence in Dr. Johnson's Gray which might well be written up in all those rooms, too humble to be called libraries, yet full of books, where the pursuit of reading is carried on by private people. " . . . I rejoice to concur with the common reader; for by the common sense of readers, uncorrupted by literary prejudices, after all the refinements of subtilty and the dogmatism of learning, must be finally decided all claim to poetical honours." It defines their qualities; it dignifies their aims; it bestows upon a pursuit which devours a great deal of time, and is yet apt to leave behind it nothing very substantial, the sanction of the great man's approval.

The common reader, as Dr. Johnson implies, differs from the critic and the scholar. He is worse educated, and nature has not gifted him so generously. He reads for his own pleasure rather than to impart knowledge or correct the opinions of others. Above all, he is guided by an instinct to create for himself, out of whatever odds and ends he can come by, some kind of whole--a portrait of a man, a sketch of an age, a theory of the art of writing. He never ceases, as he reads, to run up some rickety and ramshackle fabric which shall give him the temporary satisfaction of looking sufficiently like the real object to allow of affection, laughter, and argument. Hasty, inaccurate, and superficial, snatching now this poem, now that scrap of old furniture, without caring where he finds it or of what nature it may be so long as it serves his purpose and rounds his structure, his deficiencies as a critic are too obvious to be pointed out; but if he has, as Dr. Johnson maintained, some say in the final distribution of poetical honours, then, perhaps, it may be worth while to write down a few of the ideas and opinions which, insignificant in themselves, yet contribute to so mighty a result.

"JANE EYRE" AND "WUTHERING HEIGHTS"

Of the hundred years that have passed since Charlotte Bronte was born, she, the centre now of so much legend, devotion, and literature, lived but thirty-nine. It is strange to reflect how different those legends might have been had her life reached the ordinary human span. She might have become, like some of her famous contemporaries, a figure familiarly met with in London and elsewhere, the subject of pictures and anecdotes innumerable, the writer of many novels, of memoirs possibly, removed from us well within the memory of the middle-aged in all the splendour of established fame. She might have been wealthy, she might have been prosperous. But it is not so. When we think of her we have to imagine some one who had no lot in our modern world; we have to cast our minds back to the 'fifties of the last century, to a remote parsonage upon the wild Yorkshire moors. In that parsonage, and on those moors, unhappy and lonely, in her poverty and her exaltation, she remains for ever.

These circumstances, as they affected her character, may have left their traces on her work. A novelist, we reflect, is bound to build up his structure with much very perishable material which begins by lending it reality and ends by cumbering it with rubbish. As we open JAYNE EYRE once more we cannot stifle the suspicion that we shall find her world of imagination as antiquated, mid-Victorian, and out of date as the parsonage on the moor, a place only to be visited by the curious, only preserved by the pious. So we open JAYNE EYRE; and in two pages every doubt is swept clean from our minds.

Folds of scarlet drapery shut in my view to the right hand; to the left were the clear panes of glass, protecting, but not separating me from the drear November day. At intervals, while turning over the leaves of my book, I studied the aspect of that winter afternoon. Afar, it offered a pale blank of mist and cloud; near, a scene of wet lawn and storm-beat shrub, with ceaseless rain sweeping away wildly before a long and lamentable blast.

There is nothing there more perishable than the moor itself, or more subject to the sway of fashion than the "long and lamentable blast". Nor is this exhilaration short-lived. It rushes us through the entire volume, without giving us time to think, without letting us lift our eyes from the page. So intense is our absorption that if some one moves in the room the movement seems to take place not there but up in Yorkshire. The writer has us by the hand, forces us along her road, makes us see what she sees, never leaves us for a moment or allows us to forget her. At the end we are steeped through and through with the genius, the vehemence, the indignation of Charlotte Bronte. Remarkable faces, figures of strong outline and gnarled feature have flashed upon us in passing; but it is through her eyes that we have seen them. Once she is gone, we seek for them in vain. Think of Rochester and we have to think of JAYNE EYRE. Think of the moor, and again there is JAYNE EYRE. Think of the drawing-room, [Note, below] even, those "white carpets on which seemed laid brilliant garlands of flowers", that "pale Parian mantelpiece" with its Bohemia glass of "ruby red" and the "general blending of snow and fire"--what is all that except JAYNE EYRE?

[Note: Charlotte and Emily Brontë had much the same sense of colour. ". . . we saw--ah! it was beautiful--a splendid place carpeted with crimson, and crimson-covered chairs and tables, and a pure white ceiling bordered by gold, a shower of glass drops hanging in silver chains from the centre, and shimmering with little soft tapers " (WUTHERING HEIGHTS). "Yet it was merely a very pretty drawing-room, and within it a boudoir, both spread with white carpets, on which seemed laid brilliant garlands of flowers; both ceiled with snowy mouldings of white grapes and vine leaves, beneath which glowed in rich contrast crimson couches and ottomans; while the ornaments on the pale Parian mantelpiece were of sparkling Bohemia glass, ruby red; and between the windows large mirrors repeated the general blending of snow and fire" (JANE EYRE).]

The drawbacks of being Jane Eyre are not far to seek. Always to be a governess and always to be in love is a serious limitation in a world which is full, after all, of people who are neither one nor the other. The characters of a Jane Austen or of a Tolstoi have a million facets compared with these. They live and are complex by means of their effect upon many different people who serve to mirror them in the round. They move hither and thither whether their creators watch them or not, and the world in which they live seems to us an independent world which we can visit, now that they have created it, by ourselves. Thomas Hardy is more akin to Charlotte Bronte in the power of his personality and the narrowness of his vision. But the differences are vast. As we read JUDE THE OBSCURE we are not rushed to a finish; we brood and ponder and drift away from the text in plethoric trains of thought which build up round the characters an atmosphere of question and suggestion of which they are themselves, as often as not, unconscious. Simple peasants as they are, we are forced to confront them with destinies and questionings of the hugest import, so that often it seems as if the most important characters in a Hardy novel are those which have no names. Of this power, of this speculative curiosity, Charlotte Brontë has no trace. She does not attempt to solve the problems of human life; she is even unaware that such problems exist; all her force, and it is the more tremendous for being constricted, goes into the assertion, "I love", "I hate", "I suffer".

For the self-centred and self-limited writers have a power denied the more catholic and broad-minded. Their impressions are close packed and strongly stamped between their narrow walls. Nothing issues from their minds which has not been marked with their own impress. They learn little from other writers, and what they adopt they cannot assimilate. Both Hardy and Charlotte Brontë appear to have founded their styles upon a stiff and decorous journalism. The staple of their prose is awkward and unyielding. But both with labour and the most obstinate integrity, by thinking every thought until it has subdued words to itself, have forged for themselves a prose which takes the mould of their minds entire; which has, into the bargain, a beauty, a power, a swiftness of its own. Charlotte Brontë, at least, owed nothing to the reading of many books. She never learnt the smoothness of the professional writer, or acquired his ability to stuff and sway his language as he chooses. "I could never rest in communication with strong, discreet, and refined minds, whether male or female", she writes, as any leader-writer in a provincial journal might have written; but gathering fire and speed goes on in her own authentic voice "till I had passed the outworks of conventional reserve and crossed the threshold of confidence, and won a place by their hearts' very hearthstone". It is there that she takes her seat; it is the red and fitful glow of the heart's fire which illumines her page. In other words, we read Charlotte Brontë not for exquisite observation of character--her characters are vigorous and elementary; not for comedy--hers is grim and crude; not for a philosophic view of life--hers is that of a country parson's daughter; but for her poetry. Probably that is so with all writers who have, as she has, an overpowering personality, so that, as we say in real life, they have only to open the door to make themselves felt. There is in them some untamed ferocity perpetually at war with the accepted order of things which makes them desire to create instantly rather than to observe patiently. This very ardour, rejecting half shades and other minor impediments, wings its way past the daily conduct of ordinary people and allies itself with their more inarticulate passions. It makes them poets, or, if they choose to write in prose, intolerant of its restrictions. Hence it is that both Emily and Charlotte are always invoking the help of nature. They both feel the need of some more powerful symbol of the vast and slumbering passions in human nature than words or actions can convey. It is with a description of a storm that Charlotte ends her finest novel VILLETTE. "The skies hang full and dark--a wrack sails from the west; the clouds cast themselves into strange forms." So she calls in nature to describe a state of mind which could not otherwise be expressed. But neither of the sisters observed nature accurately as Dorothy Wordsworth observed it, or painted it minutely as Tennyson painted it. They seized those aspects of the earth which were most akin to what they themselves felt or imputed to their characters, and so their storms, their moors, their lovely spaces of summer weather are not ornaments applied to decorate a dull page or display the writer's powers of observation-they carry on the emotion and light up the meaning of the book.

The meaning of a book, which lies so often apart from what happens and what is said and consists rather in some connection which things in themselves different have had for the writer, is necessarily hard to grasp. Especially this is so when, like the Brontës, the writer is poetic, and his meaning inseparable from his language, and itself rather a mood than a particular observation. WUTHERING HEIGHTS is a more difficult book to understand than JAYNE EYRE, because Emily was a greater poet than Charlotte. When

Charlotte wrote she said with eloquence and splendour and passion "I love ", "I hate", "I suffer". Her experience, though more intense, is on a level with our own. But there is no "I" in WUTHERING HEIGHTS. There are no governesses. There are no employers. There is love, but it is not the love of men and women. Emily was inspired by some more general conception. The impulse which urged her to create was not her own suffering or her own injuries. She looked out upon a world cleft into gigantic disorder and felt within her the power to unite it in a book. That gigantic ambition is to be felt throughout the novel--a struggle, half thwarted but of superb conviction, to say something through the mouths of her characters which is not merely "I love" or "I hate", but "we, the whole human race " and "you, the eternal powers . . ." the sentence remains unfinished. It is not strange that it should be so; rather it is astonishing that she can make us feel what she had it in her to say at all. It surges up in the half-articulate words of Catherine Earnshaw, "If all else perished and HE remained, I should still continue to be; and if all else remained and he were annihilated, the universe would turn to a mighty stranger; I should not seem part of it". It breaks out again in the presence of the dead. I see a repose that neither earth nor hell can break, and I feel an assurance of the endless and shadowless hereafter--the eternity they have entered--where life is boundless in its duration, and love in its sympathy and joy in its fulness." It is this suggestion of power underlying the apparitions of human nature and lifting them up into the presence of greatness that gives the book its huge stature among other novels. But it was not enough for Emily Brontë to write a few lyrics, to utter a cry, to express a creed. In her poems she did this once and for all, and her poems will perhaps outlast her novel. But she was novelist as well as poet. She must take upon herself a more laborious and a more ungrateful task. She must face the fact of other existences, grapple with the mechanism of external things, build up, in recognisable shape, farms and houses and report the speeches of men and women who existed independently of herself. And so we reach these summits of emotion not by rant or rhapsody but by hearing a girl sing old songs to herself as she rocks in the branches of a tree; by watching the moor sheep crop the turf; by listening to the soft wind breathing through the grass. The life at the farm with all its absurdities and its improbability is laid open to us. We are given every opportunity of comparing WUTHERING HEIGHTS with a real farm and Heathcliff with a real man. How, we are allowed to ask, can there be truth or insight or the finer shades of emotion in men and women who so little resemble what we have seen ourselves? But even as we ask it we see in Heathcliff the brother that a sister of genius might have seen; he is impossible we say, but nevertheless no boy in literature has a more vivid existence than his. So it is with the two Catherines; never could women feel as they do or act in their manner, we say. All the same, they are the most lovable women in English fiction. It is as if she could tear up all that we know human beings by, and fill these unrecognisable transparences with such a gust of life that they transcend reality. Hers, then, is the rarest of all powers. She could free life from its dependence on facts; with a few touches indicate the spirit of a face so that it needs no body; by speaking of the moor make the wind blow and the thunder roar

THE PATRON AND THE CROCUS

Young men and women beginning to write are generally given the plausible but utterly impracticable advice to write what they have to write as shortly as possible, as clearly as possible, and without other thought in their minds except to say exactly what is in them. Nobody ever adds on these occasions the one thing needful: "And be sure you choose your patron wisely", though that is the gist of the whole matter. For a book is always written for somebody to read, and, since the patron is not merely the paymaster, but also in a very subtle and insidious way the instigator and inspirer of what is written, it is of the utmost importance that he should be a desirable man.

But who, then, is the desirable man--the patron who will cajole the best out of the writer's brain and bring to birth the most varied and vigorous progeny of which he is capable? Different ages have answered the question differently. The Elizabethans, to speak roughly, chose the aristocracy to write for and the playhouse public. The eighteenth-century patron was a combination of coffee-house wit and Grub Street bookseller. In the nineteenth century the great writers wrote for the half-crown magazines and the leisured classes. And looking back and applauding the splendid results of these different alliances, it all seems enviably simple, and plain as a pikestaff compared with our own predicament--for whom should we write? For the present supply of patrons is of unexampled and bewildering variety. There is the daily Press, the weekly Press, the monthly Press; the English public and the American public; the best-seller public and the worst-seller public; the highbrow public and the red-blood public; all now organised self-conscious entities capable through their various mouthpieces of making their needs known and their approval or displeasure felt. Thus the writer who has been moved by the sight of the first crocus in Kensington Gardens has, before he sets pen to paper, to choose from a crowd of competitors the particular patron who suits him best. It is futile to say, "Dismiss them all; think only of your crocus", because writing is a method of communication; and the crocus is an imperfect crocus until it has been shared. The first man or the last may write for himself alone, but he is an exception and an unenviable one at that, and the gulls are welcome to his works if the gulls can read them.

Granted, then, that every writer has some public or other at the end of his pen, the high-minded will say that it should be a submissive public, accepting obediently whatever he likes to give it. Plausible as the theory sounds, great risks are attached to it. For in that case the writer remains conscious of his public, yet is superior to it--an uncomfortable and unfortunate combination, as the works of Samuel Butler, George Meredith, and Henry James may be taken to prove. Each despised the public; each desired a public; each failed to attain a public; and each wreaked his failure upon the public by a succession, gradually increasing in intensity, of angularities, obscurities, and affectations which no writer whose patron was his equal and friend would have thought it necessary to inflict. Their crocuses, in consequence, are tortured plants, beautiful and bright, but with something wry-necked about them, malformed, shrivelled on the one side, overblown on the other. A touch of the sun would have done them a world of good. Shall we then rush to the opposite extreme and accept (if in fancy alone) the flattering proposals which the editors of the Times and the Daily News may be supposed to make us--"Twenty pounds down for your crocus in precisely fifteen hundred words, which shall blossom upon every breakfast table from John o' Groats to the Land's End before nine o'clock to-morrow morning with the writer's name attached"?

But will one crocus be enough, and must it not be a very brilliant yellow to shine so far, to cost so much, and to have one's name attached to it? The Press is undoubtedly a great multiplier of crocuses. But if we look at some of these plants, we shall find that they are only very distantly related to the original little yellow or purple flower which pokes up through the grass in Kensington Gardens early in March every year. The newspaper crocus is an amazing but still a very different plant. It fills precisely the space allotted to it. It radiates a golden glow. It is genial, affable, warm-hearted. It is beautifully finished, too, for let nobody think that the art of "our dramatic critic" of the Times or of Mr. Lynd of the Daily News is an easy one. It is no despicable feat to start a million brains running at nine o'clock in the morning, to give two million eyes something bright and brisk and amusing to look at. But the night comes and these flowers fade. So little bits of glass lose their lustre if you take them out of the sea; great prima donnas howl like hyenas if you shut them up in telephone boxes; and the most brilliant of articles when removed from its element is dust and sand and the husks of straw. Journalism embalmed in a book is unreadable.

The patron we want, then, is one who will help us to preserve our flowers from decay. But as his qualities change from age to age, and it needs considerable integrity and conviction not to be dazzled by the pretensions or bamboozled by the persuasions of the competing crowd, this business of patron-finding is one of the tests and trials of authorship. To know whom to write for is to know how to write. Some of the modern patron's qualities are, however, fairly plain. The writer will require at this moment, it is obvious, a patron with the book-reading habit rather than the play-going habit. Nowadays, too, he must be instructed in the literature of other times and races. But there are other qualities which our special weaknesses and tendencies demand in him. There is the question of indecency, for instance, which plagues us and puzzles us much more than it did the Elizabethans. The twentieth-century patron must be immune from shock. He must distinguish infallibly between the little clod of manure which sticks to the crocus of necessity, and that which is plastered to it out of bravado. He must be a judge, too, of those social influences which inevitably play so large a part in modern literature, and able to say which matures and fortifies, which inhibits and makes sterile. Further, there is emotion for him to pronounce on, and in no department can he do more useful work than in bracing a writer against sentimentality on the one hand and a craven fear of expressing his feeling on the other. It is worse, he will say, and perhaps more common, to be afraid of feeling than to feel too much. He will add, perhaps, something about language, and point out how many words Shakespeare used and how much grammar Shakespeare violated, while we, though we keep our fingers so demurely to the black notes on the piano, have not appreciably improved upon ANTONY AND CLEOPATRA. And if you can forget your sex altogether, he will say, so much the better; a writer has none. But all this is by the way--elementary and disputable. The patron's prime quality is something different, only to be expressed perhaps by the use of that convenient word which cloaks so much-- atmosphere. It is necessary that the patron should shed and envelop the crocus in an atmosphere which makes it appear a plant of the very highest importance, so that to misrepresent it is the one outrage not to be forgiven this side of the grave. He must make us feel that a single crocus, if it be a real crocus, is enough for him; that he does not want to be lectured, elevated, instructed, or improved; that he is sorry that he bullied Carlyle into vociferation, Tennyson into idyllics, and Ruskin into insanity; that he is now ready to efface himself or assert himself as his writers require; that he is bound to them by a more than maternal tie; that they are twins indeed, one dying if the other dies, one flourishing if the other flourishes; that the fate of literature depends upon their happy alliance- -all of which proves, as we began by saying, that the choice of a patron is of the highest importance. But how to choose rightly? How to write well? Those are the questions.

THE MODERN ESSAY

As Mr. Rhys truly says, it is unnecessary to go profoundly into the history and origin of the essay--whether it derives from Socrates or Siranney the Persian--since, like all living things, its present is more important than its past. Moreover, the family is widely spread; and while some of its representatives have risen in the world and wear their coronets with the best, others pick up a precarious living in the gutter near Fleet Street. The form, too, admits variety. The essay can be short or long, serious or trifling, about God and Spinoza, or about turtles and Cheapside. But as we turn over the pages of these five little volumes, [MODEM ENGLISH ESSAYS, edited by Ernest Rhys, 5 vols. (Dent).] containing essays written between 1870 and 1920, certain principles appear to control the chaos, and we detect in the short period under review something like the progress of history.

Of all forms of literature, however, the essay is the one which least calls for the use of long words. The principle which controls it is simply that it should give pleasure; the desire which impels us when we take it from the shelf is simply to receive pleasure. Everything in an essay must be subdued to that end. It should lay us under a spell with its first word, and we should only wake, refreshed, with its last. In the interval we may pass through the most various experiences of amusement, surprise, interest, indignation; we may soar to the heights of fantasy with Lamb or plunge to the depths of wisdom with Bacon, but we must never be roused. The essay must lap us about and draw its curtain across the world.

So great a feat is seldom accomplished, though the fault may well be as much on the reader's side as on the writer's. Habit and lethargy have dulled his palate. A novel has a story, a poem rhyme; but what art can the essayist use in these short lengths of prose to sting us wide awake and fix us in a trance which is not sleep but rather an intensification of life--a basking, with every faculty alert, in the sun of pleasure? He must know--that is the first essential--how to write. His learning may be as profound as Mark Pattison's, but in an essay it must be so fused by the magic of writing that not a fact juts out, not a dogma tears the surface of the texture. Macaulay in one way, Froude in another, did this superbly over and over again. They have blown more knowledge into us in the course of one essay than the innumerable chapters of a hundred text-books. But when Mark Pattison has to tell us, in the space of thirty-five little pages, about Montaigne, we feel that he had not previously assimilated M. Grün. M. Grün was a gentleman who once wrote a bad book. M. Grün and his book should have been embalmed for our perpetual delight in amber. But the process is fatiguing; it requires more time and perhaps more temper than Pattison had at his command. He served M. Grün up raw, and he remains a crude berry among the cooked meats, upon which our teeth must grate for ever. Something of the sort applies to Matthew Arnold and a certain translator of Spinoza. Literal truth-telling and finding fault with a culprit for his good are out of place in an essay, where everything should be for our good and rather for eternity than for the March number of the FORTNIGHTLY REVIEW. But if the voice of the scold should never be heard in this narrow plot, there is another voice which is as a plague of locusts--the voice of a man stumbling drowsily among loose words, clutching aimlessly at vague ideas, the voice, for example, of Mr. Hutton in the following passage:

Add to this that his married life was very brief, only seven years and a half, being unexpectedly cut short, and that his passionate reverence for his wife's memory and genius--in his own words, "a religion"--was one which, as he must have been perfectly sensible, he could not make to appear otherwise than extravagant, not to say an hallucination, in the eyes of the rest of mankind, and yet that he was possessed by an irresistible yearning to attempt to embody it in all the tender and enthusiastic hyperbole of which it is so pathetic to find a man who gained his fame by his "dry-light" a master, and it is impossible not to feel that the human incidents in Mr. Mill's career are very sad.

A book could take that blow, but it sinks an essay. A biography in two volumes is indeed the proper depository; for there, where the licence is so much wider, and hints and glimpses of outside things make part of the feast (we refer to the old type of Victorian volume), these yawns and stretches hardly matter, and have indeed some positive value of their own. But that value, which is contributed by the reader, perhaps illicitly, in his desire to get as much into the book from all possible sources as he can, must be ruled out here.

There is no room for the impurities of literature in an essay. Somehow or other, by dint of labour or bounty of nature, or both combined, the essay must be pure--pure like water or pure like wine, but pure from dullness, deadness, and deposits of extraneous matter. Of all writers in the first volume, Walter Pater best achieves this arduous task, because before setting out to write his essay ("Notes on Leonardo da Vinci") he has somehow contrived to get his material fused. He is a learned man, but it is not knowledge of Leonardo that remains with us, but a vision, such as we get in a good novel where everything contributes to bring the writer's conception as a whole before us. Only here, in the essay, where the bounds are so strict and facts have to be used in their nakedness, the true writer like Walter Pater makes these limitations yield their own quality. Truth will give it authority; from its narrow limits he will get shape and intensity; and then there is no more fitting place for some of those ornaments which the old writers loved and we, by calling them ornaments, presumably despise. Nowadays nobody would have the courage to embark on the once famous description of Leonardo's lady who has

learned the secrets of the grave; and has been a diver in deep seas and keeps their fallen day about her; and trafficked for strange webs with Eastern merchants; and, as Leda, was the mother of Helen of Troy, and, as Saint Anne, the mother of Mary. . . .

The passage is too thumb-marked to slip naturally into the context. But when we come unexpectedly upon "the smiling of women and the motion of great waters", or upon "full of the refinement of the dead, in sad, earth-coloured raiment, set with pale stones", we suddenly remember that we have ears and we have eyes, and that the English language fills a long array of stout volumes with innumerable words, many of which are of more than one syllable. The only living Englishman who ever looks into these volumes is, of course, a gentleman of Polish extraction. But doubtless our abstention saves us much gush, much rhetoric, much high-stepping and cloud-prancing, and for the sake of the prevailing sobriety and hard-headedness we should be willing to barter the splendour of Sir Thomas Browne and the vigour of Swift.

Yet, if the essay admits more properly than biography or fiction of sudden boldness and metaphor, and can be polished till every atom of its surface shines, there are dangers in that too. We are soon in sight of ornament. Soon the current, which is the life-blood of literature, runs slow; and instead of sparkling and flashing or moving with a quieter impulse which has a deeper excitement, words coagulate together in frozen sprays which, like the grapes on a Christmas-tree, glitter for a single night, but are dusty and garish the day after. The temptation to decorate is great where the theme may be of the slightest. What is there to interest another in the fact that one has enjoyed a walking tour, or has amused oneself by rambling down Cheapside and looking at the turtles in Mr. Sweeting's shop window? Stevenson and Samuel Butler chose very different methods of exciting our interest in these domestic themes. Stevenson, of course, trimmed and polished and set out his matter in the traditional eighteenth-century form. It is admirably done, but we cannot help feeling anxious, as the essay proceeds, lest the material may give out under the craftsman's fingers. The ingot is so small, the manipulation so incessant. And perhaps that is why the peroration

To sit still and contemplate--to remember the faces of women without desire, to be pleased by the great deeds of men without envy, to be everything and everywhere in sympathy and yet content to remain where and what you are

has the sort of insubstantiality which suggests that by the time he got to the end he had left himself nothing solid to work with. Butler adopted the very opposite method. Think your own thoughts, he seems to say, and speak them as plainly as you can. These turtles in the shop window which appear to leak out of their shells through heads and feet suggest a fatal faithfulness to a fixed idea. And so, striding unconcernedly from one idea to the next, we traverse a large stretch of ground; observe that a wound in the solicitor is a very serious thing; that Mary Queen of Scots wears surgical boots and is subject to fits near the Horse Shoe in Tottenham Court Road; take it for granted that no one really cares about Aeschylus; and so, with many amusing anecdotes and some profound reflections, reach the peroration, which is that, as he had been told not to see more in Cheapside than he could get into twelve pages of the Universal Review, he had better stop. And yet obviously Butler is at least as careful of our pleasure as Stevenson; and to write like oneself and call it not writing is a much harder exercise in style than to write like Addison and call it writing well.

But, however much they differ individually, the Victorian essayists yet had something in common. They wrote at greater length than is now usual, and they wrote for a public which had not only time to sit down to its magazine seriously, but a high, if peculiarly Victorian, standard of culture by which to judge it. It was worth while to speak out upon serious matters in an essay; and there was nothing absurd in writing as well as one possibly could when, in a month or two, the same public which had welcomed the essay in a magazine would carefully read it once more in a book. But a change came from a small audience of cultivated people to a larger audience of people who were not quite so cultivated. The change was not altogether for the worse. In volume iii. we find Mr. Birrell and Mr. Beerbohm. It might even be said that there was a reversion to the classic type, and that the essay by losing its size and something of its sonority was approaching more nearly the essay of Addison and Lamb. At any rate, there is a great gulf between Mr. Birrell on Carlyle and the essay which one may suppose that Carlyle would have written upon Mr. Birrell. There is little similarity between A CLOUD OF PINAFORES, by Max Beerbohm, and A CYNIC'S APOLOGY, by Leslie Stephen. But the essay is alive; there is no reason to despair. As the conditions change so the essayist, most sensitive of all plants to public opinion, adapts himself, and if he is good makes the best of the change, and if he is bad the worst. Mr. Birrell is certainly good; and so we find that, though he has dropped a considerable amount of weight, his attack is much more direct and his movement more supple. But what did Mr. Beerbohm give to the essay and what did he take from it? That is a much more complicated question, for here we have an essayist who has concentrated on the work and is without doubt the prince of his profession.

What Mr. Beerbohm gave was, of course, himself. This presence, which has haunted the essay fitfully from the time of Montaigne, had been in exile since the death of Charles Lamb. Matthew Arnold was never to his readers Matt, nor Walter Pater affectionately abbreviated in a thousand homes to Wat. They gave us much, but that they did not give. Thus, some time in the nineties, it must have surprised readers accustomed to exhortation, information, and denunciation to find themselves familiarly addressed by a voice which seemed to belong to a man no larger than themselves. He was affected by private joys and sorrows, and had no gospel to preach and no learning to impart. He was himself, simply and directly, and himself he has remained. Once again we have an essayist capable of using the essayist's most proper but most dangerous and delicate tool. He has brought personality into literature, not unconsciously and impurely, but so consciously and purely that we do not know whether there is any relation between Max the essayist and Mr. Beerbohm the man. We only know that the spirit of personality permeates every word that he writes. The triumph is the triumph of style. For it is only by knowing how to write that you can make use in literature of your self; that self which, while it is essential to literature, is also its most dangerous antagonist. Never to be yourself and yet always--that is the problem. Some of the essayists in Mr. Rhys' collection, to be frank, have not altogether succeeded in solving it. We are nauseated by the sight of trivial personalities decomposing in the eternity of print. As talk, no doubt, it was charming, and certainly the writer is a good fellow to meet over a bottle of beer. But literature is stern; it is no use being charming, virtuous, or even learned and brilliant into the bargain, unless, she seems to reiterate, you fulfil her first condition--to know how to write.

This art is possessed to perfection by Mr. Beerbohm. But he has not searched the dictionary for polysyllables. He has not moulded firm periods or seduced our ears with intricate cadences and strange melodies. Some of his companions--Henley and Stevenson, for example--are momentarily more impressive. But A CLOUD OF PINAFORES has in it that indescribable inequality, stir, and final expressiveness which belong to life and to life alone. You have not finished with it because you have read it, any more than friendship is ended because it is time to part. Life wells up and alters and adds. Even things in a book-case change if they are alive; we find ourselves wanting to meet them again; we find them altered. So we look back upon essay after essay by Mr. Beerbohm, knowing that, come September or May, we shall sit down with them and talk. Yet it is true that the essayist is the most sensitive of all writers to public opinion. The drawing-room is the place where a great deal of reading is done nowadays, and the essays of Mr. Beerbohm lie, with an exquisite appreciation of all that the position exacts, upon the drawing-room table. There is no gin about; no strong tobacco; no puns, drunkenness, or insanity. Ladies and gentlemen talk together, and some things, of course, are not said.

But if it would be foolish to attempt to confine Mr. Beerbohm to one room, it would be still more foolish, unhappily, to make him, the artist, the man who gives us only his best, the representative of our age. There are no essays by Mr. Beerbohm in the fourth or fifth volumes of the present collection. His age seems already a little distant, and the drawing-room table, as it recedes, begins to look rather like an altar where, once upon a time, people deposited offerings--fruit from their own orchards, gifts carved with their own hands. Now once more the conditions have changed. The public needs essays as much as ever, and perhaps even more. The demand for the light middle not exceeding fifteen hundred words, or in special cases seventeen hundred and fifty, much exceeds the supply. Where Lamb wrote one essay and Max perhaps writes two, Mr. Belloc at a rough computation produces three hundred and sixty-five. They are very short, it is true. Yet with what dexterity the practised essayist will utilise his space--beginning as close to the top of the sheet as possible, judging precisely how far to go, when to turn, and how, without sacrificing a hair's-breadth of paper, to wheel about and alight accurately upon the last word his editor allows! As a feat of skill it is well worth watching. But the personality upon which Mr. Belloc, like Mr. Beerbohm, depends suffers in the process. It comes to us not with the natural richness of the speaking voice, but strained and thin and full of mannerisms and affectations, like the voice of a man shouting through a megaphone to a crowd on a windy day. "Little friends, my readers", he says in the essay called "An Unknown Country", and he goes on to tell us how

There was a shepherd the other day at Findon Fair who had come from the east by Lewes with sheep, and who had in his eyes that reminiscence of horizons which makes the eyes of shepherds and of mountaineers different from the eyes of other men. . . . I went with him to hear what he had to say, for shepherds talk quite differently from other men.

Happily this shepherd had little to say, even under the stimulus of the inevitable mug of beer, about the Unknown Country, for the only remark that he did make proves him either a minor poet, unfit for the care of sheep, or Mr. Belloc himself masquerading with a fountain pen. That is the penalty which the habitual essayist must now be prepared to face. He must masquerade. He cannot afford the time either to be himself or to be other people. He must skim the surface of thought and dilute the strength of personality. He must give us a worn weekly halfpenny instead of a solid sovereign once a year.

But it is not Mr. Belloc only who has suffered from the prevailing conditions. The essays which bring the collection to the year 1920 may not be the best of their authors' work, but, if we except writers like Mr. Conrad and Mr. Hudson, who have strayed into essay writing accidentally, and concentrate upon those who write essays habitually, we shall find them a good deal affected by the change in their circumstances. To write weekly, to write daily, to write shortly, to write for busy people catching trains in the morning or for tired people coming home in the evening, is a heart-breaking task for men who know good writing from bad. They do it, but instinctively draw out of harm's way anything precious that might be damaged by contact with the public, or anything sharp that might irritate its skin. And so, if one reads Mr. Lucas, Mr. Lynd, or Mr. Squire in the bulk, one feels that a common greyness silvers everything. They are as far removed from the extravagant beauty of Walter Pater as they are from the intemperate candour of Leslie Stephen. Beauty and courage are dangerous spirits to bottle in a column and a half; and thought, like a brown paper parcel in a waistcoat pocket, has a way of spoiling the symmetry of an article. It is a kind, tired, apathetic world for which they write, and the marvel is that they never cease to attempt, at least, to write well.

But there is no need to pity Mr. Clutton Brock for this change in the essayist's conditions. He has clearly made the best of his circumstances and not the worst. One hesitates even to say that he has had to make any conscious effort in the matter, so naturally has he effected the transition from the private essayist to the public, from the drawing-room to the Albert Hall. Paradoxically enough, the shrinkage in size has brought about a corresponding expansion of individuality.

We have no longer the "I" of Max and of Lamb, but the "we" of public bodies and other sublime personages. It is "we" who go to hear the MAGIC FLUTE; "we" who ought to profit by it; "we", in some mysterious way, who, in our corporate capacity, once upon a time actually wrote it. For music and literature and art must submit to the same generalisation or they will not carry to the farthest recesses of the Albert Hall. That the voice of Mr. Clutton Brock, so sincere and so disinterested, carries such a distance and reaches so many without pandering to the weakness of the mass or its passions must be a matter of legitimate satisfaction to us all. But while "we" are gratified, "I", that unruly partner in the human fellowship, is reduced to despair. "I" must always think things for himself, and feel things for himself. To share them in a diluted form with the majority of well-educated and well-intentioned men and women is for him sheer agony; and while the rest of us listen intently and profit profoundly, "I" slips off to the woods and the fields and rejoices in a single blade of grass or a solitary potato.

In the fifth volume of modern essays, it seems, we have got some way from pleasure and the art of writing. But in justice to the essayists of 1920 we must be sure that we are not praising the famous because they have been praised already and the dead because we shall never meet them wearing spats in Piccadilly. We must know what we mean when we say that they can write and give us pleasure. We must compare them; we must bring out the quality. We must point to this and say it is good because it is exact, truthful, and imaginative:

Nay, retire men cannot when they would; neither will they, when it were Reason; but are impatient of Privateness, even in age and sickness, which require the shadow: like old Townsmen: that will still he sitting at their street door, though therby they offer Age to Scorn . . .

and to this, and say it is bad because it is loose, plausible, and commonplace:

With courteous and precise cynicism on his lips, he thought of quiet virginal chambers, of waters singing under the moon, of terraces where taintless music sobbed into the open night, of pure maternal mistresses with protecting arms and vigilant eyes, of fields slumbering in the sunlight, of leagues of ocean heaving under warm tremulous heavens, of hot ports, gorgeous and perfumed. . .

It goes on, but already we are bemused with sound and neither feel nor hear. The comparison makes us suspect that the art of writing has for backbone some fierce attachment to an idea. It is on the back of an idea, something believed in with conviction or seen with precision and thus compelling words to its shape, that the diverse company which includes Lamb and Bacon, and Mr. Beerbohm and Hudson, and Vernon Lee and Mr. Conrad, and Leslie Stephen and Butler and Walter Pater reaches the farther shore. Very various talents have helped or hindered the passage of the idea into words. Some scrape through painfully; others fly with every wind favouring. But Mr. Belloc and Mr. Lucas and Mr. Squire are not fiercely attached to anything in itself. They share the contemporary dilemma--that lack of an obstinate conviction which lifts ephemeral sounds through the misty sphere of anybody's language to the land where there is a perpetual marriage, a perpetual union. Vague as all definitions are, a good essay must have this permanent quality about it; it must draw its curtain round us but it must be a curtain that shuts us in, not out.

THE DEATH OF THE MOTH

Moths that fly by day are not properly to be called moths; they do not excite that pleasant sense of dark autumn nights and ivy-blossom which the commonest yellow-underwing asleep in the shadow of the curtain never fails to rouse in us. They are hybrid creatures, neither gay like butterflies nor sombre like their own species. Nevertheless the present specimen, with his narrow hay-coloured wings, fringed with a tassel of the same colour, seemed to be content with life. It was a pleasant morning, mid-September, mild, benignant, yet with a keener breath than that of the summer months. The plough was already scoring the field opposite the window, and where the share had been, the earth was pressed flat and gleamed with moisture. Such vigour came rolling in from the fields and the down beyond that it was difficult to keep the eyes strictly turned upon the book. The rooks too were keeping one of their annual festivities; soaring round the tree tops until it looked as if a vast net with thousands of black knots in it had been cast up into the air; which, after a few moments sank slowly down upon the trees until every twig seemed to have a knot at the end of it. Then, suddenly, the net would be thrown into the air again in a wider circle this time, with the utmost clamour and vociferation, as though to be thrown into the air and settle slowly down upon the tree tops were a tremendously exciting experience.

The same energy which inspired the rooks, the ploughmen, the horses, and even, it seemed, the lean bare-backed downs, sent the moth fluttering from side to side of his square of the window-pane. One could not help watching him. One was, indeed, conscious of a queer feeling of pity for him. The possibilities of pleasure seemed that morning so enormous and so various that to have only a moth's part in life, and a day moth's at that, appeared a hard fate, and his zest in enjoying his meagre opportunities to the full, pathetic. He flew vigorously to one corner of his compartment, and, after waiting there a second, flew across to the other. What remained for him but to fly to a third corner and then to a fourth? That was all he could do, in spite of the size of the downs, the width of the sky, the far-off smoke of houses, and the romantic voice, now and then, of a steamer out at sea. What he could do he did. Watching him, it seemed as if a fibre, very thin but pure, of the enormous energy of the world had been thrust into his frail and diminutive body. As often as he crossed the pane, I could fancy that a thread of vital light became visible. He was little or nothing but life.

Yet, because he was so small, and so simple a form of the energy that was rolling in at the open window and driving its way through so many narrow and intricate corridors in my own brain and in those of other human beings, there was something marvellous as well as pathetic about him. It was as if someone had taken a tiny bead of pure life and decking it as lightly as possible with down and feathers, had set it dancing and zig-zagging to show us the true nature of life. Thus displayed one could not get over the strangeness of it. One is apt to forget all about life, seeing it humped and bossed and garnished and cumbered so that it has to move with the greatest circumspection and dignity. Again, the thought of all that life might have been had he been born in any other shape caused one to view his simple activities with a kind of pity.

After a time, tired by his dancing apparently, he settled on the window ledge in the sun, and, the queer spectacle being at an end, I forgot about him. Then, looking up, my eye was caught by him. He was trying to resume his dancing, but seemed either so stiff or so awkward that he could only flutter to the bottom of the window-pane; and when he tried to fly across it he failed. Being intent on other matters I watched these futile attempts for a time without thinking, unconsciously waiting for him to resume his flight, as one waits for a machine, that has stopped momentarily, to start again without considering the reason of its failure. After perhaps a seventh attempt he slipped from the wooden ledge and fell, fluttering his wings, on to his back on the window sill. The helplessness of his attitude roused me. It flashed upon me that he was in difficulties; he could no longer raise himself; his legs struggled vainly. But, as I stretched out a pencil, meaning to help him to right himself, it came over me that the failure and awkwardness were the approach of death. I laid the pencil down again.

The legs agitated themselves once more. I looked as if for the enemy against which he struggled. I looked out of doors. What had happened there? Presumably it was midday, and work in the fields had stopped. Stillness and quiet had replaced the previous animation. The birds had taken themselves off to feed in the brooks. The horses stood still. Yet the power was there all the same, massed outside indifferent, impersonal, not attending to anything in particular. Somehow it was opposed to the little hay-coloured moth. It was useless to try to do anything. One could only watch the extraordinary efforts made by those tiny legs against an oncoming doom which could, had it chosen, have submerged an entire city, not merely a city, but masses of human beings; nothing, I knew, had any chance against death. Nevertheless after a pause of exhaustion the legs fluttered again. It was superb this last protest, and so frantic that he succeeded at last in righting himself. One's sympathies, of course, were all on the side of life. Also, when there was nobody to care or to know, this gigantic effort on the part of an insignificant little moth, against a power of such magnitude, to retain what no one else valued or desired to keep, moved one strangely. Again, somehow, one saw life, a pure bead. I lifted the pencil again, useless though I knew it to be. But even as I did so, the unmistakable tokens of death showed themselves. The body relaxed, and instantly grew stiff. The struggle was over. The insignificant little creature now knew death. As I looked at the dead moth, this minute wayside triumph of so great a force over so mean an antagonist filled me with wonder. Just as life had been strange a few minutes before, so death was now as strange. The moth having righted himself now lay most decently and uncomplainingly composed. O yes, he seemed to say, death is stronger than I am.

EVENING OVER SUSSEX: REFLECTIONS IN A MOTOR CAR

Evening is kind to Sussex, for Sussex is no longer young, and she is grateful for the veil of evening as an elderly woman is glad when a shade is drawn over a lamp, and only the outline of her face remains. The outline of Sussex is still very fine. The cliffs stand out to sea, one behind another. All Eastbourne, all Bexhill, all St. Leonards, their parades and their lodging houses, their bead shops and their sweet shops and their placards and their invalids and chars-á-bancs, are all obliterated. What remains is what there was when William came over from France ten centuries ago: a line of cliffs running out to sea. Also the fields are redeemed. The freckle of red villas on the coast is washed over by a thin lucid lake of brown air, in which they and their redness are drowned. It was still too early for lamps; and too early for stars.

But, I thought, there is always some sediment of irritation when the moment is as beautiful as it is now. The psychologists must explain; one looks up, one is overcome by beauty extravagantly greater than one could expect--there are now pink clouds over Battle; the fields are mottled, marbled--one's perceptions blow out rapidly like air balls expanded by some rush of air, and then, when all seems blown to its fullest and tautest, with beauty and beauty and beauty, a pin pricks; it collapses. But what is the pin? So far as I could tell, the pin had something to do with one's own impotency. I cannot hold this--I cannot express this--I am overcome by it--I am mastered. Somewhere in that region one's discontent lay; and it was allied with the idea that one's nature demands mastery over all that it receives; and mastery here meant the power to convey what one saw now over Sussex so that another person could share it. And further, there was another prick of the pin: one was wasting one's chance; for beauty spread at one's right hand, at one's left; at one's back too; it was escaping all the time; one could only offer a thimble to a torrent that could fill baths, lakes.

But relinquish, I said (it is well known how in circumstances like these the self splits up and one self is eager and dissatisfied and the other stern and philosophical), relinquish these impossible aspirations; be content with the view in front of us, and believe me when I tell you that it is best to sit and soak; to be passive; to accept; and do not bother because nature has given you six little pocket knives with which to cut up the body of a whale.

While these two selves then held a colloquy about the wise course to adopt in the presence of beauty, I (a third party now declared itself) said to myself, how happy they were to enjoy so simple an occupation. There they sat as the car sped along, noticing everything: a hay stack; a rust red roof; a pond; an old man coming home with his sack on his back; there they sat, matching every colour in the sky and earth from their colour box, rigging up little models of Sussex barns and farmhouses in the red light that would serve in the January gloom. But I, being somewhat different, sat aloof and melancholy. While they are thus busied, I said to myself: Gone, gone; over, over; past and done with, past and done with. I feel life left behind even as the road is left behind. We have been over that stretch, and are already forgotten. There, windows were lit by our lamps for a second; the light is out now. Others come behind us.

Then suddenly a fourth self (a self which lies in ambush, apparently dormant, and jumps upon one unawares. Its remarks are often entirely disconnected with what has been happening, but must be attended to because of their very abruptness) said: "Look at that." It was a light; brilliant, freakish; inexplicable. For a second I was unable to name it. "A star"; and for that second it held its odd flicker of unexpectedness and danced and beamed. "I take your meaning," I said. "You, erratic and impulsive self that you are, feel that the light over the downs there emerging, dangles from the future. Let us try to understand this. Let us reason it out. I feel suddenly attached not to the past but to the future. I think of Sussex in five hundred years to come. I think much grossness will have evaporated. Things will have been scorched up, eliminated. There will be magic gates. Draughts fan-blown by electric power will cleanse houses. Lights intense and firmly directed will go over the earth, doing the work. Look at the moving light in that hill; it is the headlight of a car. By day and by night Sussex in five centuries will be full of charming thoughts, quick, effective beams."

The sun was now low beneath the horizon. Darkness

spread rapidly. None of my selves could see anything beyond the tapering light of our headlamps on the hedge. I summoned them together. "Now," I said, "comes the season of making up our accounts. Now we have got to collect ourselves; we have got to be one self. Nothing is to be seen any more, except one wedge of road and bank which our lights repeat incessantly. We are perfectly provided for. We are warmly wrapped in a rug; we are protected from wind and rain. We are alone. Now is the time of reckoning. Now I, who preside over the company, am going to arrange in order the trophies which we have all brought in. Let me see; there was a great deal of beauty brought in to-day: farmhouses; cliffs standing out to sea; marbled fields; mottled fields; red feathered skies; all that. Also there was disappearance and the death of the individual. The vanishing road and the window lit for a second and then dark. And then there was the sudden dancing light, that was hung in the future. What we have made then to-day," I said, "is this: that beauty; death of the individual; and the future. Look, I will make a little figure for your satisfaction; here he comes. Does this little figure advancing through beauty, through death, to the economical, powerful and efficient future when houses will be cleansed by a puff of hot wind satisfy you? Look at him; there on my knee." We sat and looked at the figure we had made that day. Great sheer slabs of rock, tree tufted, surrounded him. He was for a second very, very solemn. Indeed it seemed as if the reality of things were displayed there on the rug. A violent thrill ran through us; as if a charge of electricity had entered in to us. We cried out together: "Yes, yes," as if affirming something, in a moment of recognition.

And then the body who had been silent up to now began its song, almost at first as low as the rush of the wheels: "Eggs and bacon; toast and tea; fire and a bath; fire and a bath; jugged hare," it went on, "and red currant jelly; a glass of wine with coffee to follow, with coffee to follow--and then to bed and then to bed."

"Off with you," I said to my assembled selves. "Your work is done. I dismiss you. Good-night."

And the rest of the journey was performed in the delicious society of my own body.

THREE PICTURES (Written in June 1929.)
THE FIRST PICTURE

It is impossible that one should not see pictures; because if my father was a blacksmith and yours was a peer of the realm, we must needs be pictures to each other. We cannot possibly break out of the frame of the picture by speaking natural words. You see me leaning against the door of the smithy with a horseshoe in my hand and you think as you go by: "How picturesque!" I, seeing you sitting so much at your ease in the car, almost as if you were going to bow to the populace, think what a picture of old luxurious aristocratical England! We are both quite wrong in our judgments no doubt, but that is inevitable.

So now at the turn of the road I saw one of these pictures. It might have been called "The Sailor's Homecoming" or some such title. A fine young sailor carrying a bundle; a girl with her hand on his arm; neighbours gathering round; a cottage garden ablaze with flowers; as one passed one read at the bottom of that picture that the sailor was back from China, and there was a fine spread waiting for him in the parlour; and he had a present for his young wife in his bundle; and she was soon going to bear him their first child. Everything was right and good and as it should be, one felt about that picture.

There was something wholesome and satisfactory in the sight of such happiness; life seemed sweeter and more enviable than before.

So thinking I passed them, filling in the picture as fully, as completely as I could, noticing the colour of her dress, of his eyes, seeing the sandy cat slinking round the cottage door.

For some time the picture floated in my eyes, making most things appear much brighter, warmer, and simpler than usual; and making some things appear foolish; and some things wrong and some things right, and more full of meaning than before. At odd moments during that day and the next the picture returned to one's mind, and one thought with envy, but with kindness, of the happy sailor and his wife; one wondered what they were doing, what they were saying now. The imagination supplied other pictures springing from that first one, a picture of the sailor cutting firewood, drawing water; and they talked about China; and the girl set his present on the chimney-piece where everyone who came could see it; and she sewed at her baby clothes, and all the doors and windows were open into the garden so that the birds were flittering and the bees humming, and Rogers-- that was his name--could not say how much to his liking all this was after the China seas. As he smoked his pipe, with his foot in the garden.

THE SECOND PICTURE

In the middle of the night a loud cry rang through the village. Then there was a sound of something scuffling; and then dead silence. All that could be seen out of the window was the branch of lilac tree hanging motionless and ponderous across the road. It was a hot still night. There was no moon. The cry made everything seem ominous. Who had cried? Why had she cried? It was a woman's voice, made by some extremity of feeling almost sexless, almost expressionless. It was as if human nature had cried out against some iniquity, some inexpressible horror. There was dead silence. The stars shone perfectly steadily. The fields lay still. The trees were motionless. Yet all seemed guilty, convicted, ominous. One felt that something ought to be done. Some light ought to appear tossing, moving agitatedly. Someone ought to come running down the road. There should be lights in the cottage windows. And then perhaps another cry, but less sexless, less wordless, comforted, appeased. But no light came. No feet were heard. There was no second cry. The first had been swallowed up, and there was dead silence.

One lay in the dark listening intently. It had been merely a voice. There was nothing to connect it with. No picture of any sort came to interpret it, to make it intelligible to the mind. But as the dark arose at last all one saw was an obscure human form, almost without shape, raising a gigantic arm in vain against some overwhelming iniquity.

THE THIRD PICTURE

The fine weather remained unbroken. Had it not been for that single cry in the night one would have felt that the earth had put into harbour; that life had ceased to drive before the wind; that it had reached some quiet cove and there lay anchored, hardly moving, on the quiet waters. But the sound persisted. Wherever one went, it might be for a long walk up into the hills, something seemed to turn uneasily beneath the surface, making the peace, the stability all round one seem a little unreal. There were the sheep clustered on the side of the hill; the valley broke in long tapering waves like the fall of smooth waters. One came on solitary farmhouses. The puppy rolled in the yard. The butterflies gambolled over the gorse. All was as quiet, as safe could be. Yet, one kept thinking, a cry had rent it; all this beauty had been an accomplice that night; had consented; to remain calm, to be still beautiful; at any moment it might be sundered again. This goodness, this safety were only on the surface.

And then to cheer oneself out of this apprehensive mood one turned to the picture of the sailor's homecoming. One saw it all over again producing various little details-- the blue colour of her dress, the shadow that fell from the yellow flowering tree--that one had not used before. So they had stood at the cottage door, he with his bundle on his back, she just lightly touching his sleeve with her hand. And a sandy cat had slunk round the door. Thus gradually going over the picture in every detail, one persuaded oneself by degrees that it was far more likely that this calm and content and good will lay beneath the surface than anything treacherous, sinister. The sheep grazing, the waves of the valley, the farmhouse, the puppy, the dancing butterflies were in fact like that all through. And so one turned back home, with one's mind fixed on the sailor and his wife, making up picture after picture of them so that one picture after another of happiness and satisfaction might be laid over that unrest, that hideous cry, until it was crushed and silenced by their pressure out of existence.

Here at last was the village, and the churchyard through which one must pass; and the usual thought came, as one entered it, of the peacefulness of the place, with its shady yews, its rubbed tombstones, its nameless graves. Death is cheerful here, one felt. Indeed, look at that picture! A man was digging a grave, and children were picnicking at the side of it while he worked. As the shovels of yellow earth were thrown up, the children were sprawling about eating bread and jam and drinking milk out of large mugs. The gravedigger's wife, a fat fair woman, had propped herself against a tombstone and spread her apron on the grass by the open grave to serve as a tea-table. Some lumps of clay had fallen among the tea things. Who was going to be buried, I asked. Had old Mr. Dodson died at last? "Oh! no. It's for young Rogers, the sailor," the woman answered, staring at me. "He died two nights ago, of some foreign fever. Didn't you hear his wife?" She rushed into the road and cried out... . "Here, Tommy, you're all covered with earth!"

What a picture it made!

OLD MRS. GREY

There are moments even in England, now, when even the busiest, most contented suddenly let fall what they hold--it may be the week's washing. Sheets and pyjamas crumble and dissolve in their hands, because, though they do not state this in so many words, it seems silly to take the washing round to Mrs. Peel when out there over the fields over the hills, there is no washing; no pinning of clothes to lines; mangling and ironing no work at all, but boundless rest. Stainless and boundless rest; space unlimited; untrodden grass; wild birds flying hills whose smooth uprise continue that wild flight.

Of all this however only seven foot by four could be seen from Mrs. Grey's corner. That was the size of her front door which stood wide open, though there was a fire burning in the grate. The fire looked like a small spot of dusty light feebly trying to escape from the embarrassing pressure of the pouring sunshine.

Mrs. Grey sat on a hard chair in the corner looking--but at what? Apparently at nothing. She did not change the focus of her eyes when visitors came in. Her eyes had ceased to focus themselves; it may be that they had lost the power. They were aged eyes, blue, unspectacled. They could see, but without looking. She had never used her eyes on anything minute and difficult; merely upon faces, and dishes and fields. And now at the age of ninety-two they saw nothing but a zigzag of pain wriggling across the door, pain that twisted her legs as it wriggled; jerked her body to and fro like a marionette. Her body was wrapped round the pain as a damp sheet is folded over a wire. The wire was spasmodically jerked by a cruel invisible hand. She flung out a foot, a hand. Then it stopped. She sat still for a moment.

In that pause she saw herself in the past at ten, at twenty, at twenty-five. She was running in and out of a cottage with eleven brothers and sisters. The line jerked. She was thrown forward in her chair.

"All dead. All dead," she mumbled. "My brothers and sisters. And my husband gone. My daughter too. But I go on. Every morning I pray God to let me pass."

The morning spread seven foot by four green and sunny. Like a fling of grain the birds settled on the land. She was jerked again by another tweak of the tormenting hand.

"I'm an ignorant old woman. I can't read or write, and every morning when I crawls down stairs, I say I wish it were night; and every night, when I crawls up to bed, I say, I wish it were day. I'm only an ignorant old woman. But I prays to God: 0 let me pass. I'm an ignorant old woman--I can't read or write."

So when the colour went out of the doorway, she could not see the other page which is then lit up; or hear the voices that have argued, sung, talked for hundreds of years.

The jerked limbs were still again.

"The doctor comes every week. The parish doctor now. Since my daughter went, we can't afford Dr. Nicholls. But he's a good man. He says he wonders I don't go. He says my heart's nothing but wind and water. Yet I don't seem able to die."

So we--humanity--insist that the body shall still cling to the wire. We put out the eyes and the ears; but we pinion it there, with a bottle of medicine, a cup of tea, a dying fire, like a rook on a barn door; but a rook that still lives, even with a nail through it.

STREET HAUNTING: A LONDON ADVENTURE
(Written in 1930.)

No one perhaps has ever felt passionately towards a lead pencil. But there are circumstances in which it can become supremely desirable to possess one; moments when we are set upon having an object, an excuse for walking half across London between tea and dinner. As the foxhunter hunts in order to preserve the breed of foxes, and the golfer plays in order that open spaces may be preserved from the builders, so when the desire comes upon us to go street rambling the pencil does for a pretext, and getting up we say: "Really I must buy a pencil," as if under cover of this excuse we could indulge safely in the greatest pleasure of town life in winter- -rambling the streets of London.

The hour should be the evening and the season winter, for in winter the champagne brightness of the air and the sociability of the streets are grateful. We are not then taunted as in the summer by the longing for shade and solitude and sweet airs from the hayfields. The evening hour, too, gives us the irresponsibility which darkness and lamplight bestow. We are no longer quite ourselves. As we step out of the house on a fine evening between four and six, we shed the self our friends know us by and become part of that vast republican army of anonymous trampers, whose society is so agreeable after the solitude of one's own room. For there we sit surrounded by objects which perpetually express the oddity of our own temperaments and enforce the memories of our own experience. That bowl on the mantelpiece, for instance, was bought at Mantua on a windy day. We were leaving the shop when the sinister old woman plucked at our skirts and said she would find herself starving one of these days, but, "Take it!" she cried, and thrust the blue and white china bowl into our hands as if she never wanted to be reminded of her quixotic generosity. So, guiltily, but suspecting nevertheless how badly we had been fleeced, we carried it back to the little hotel where, in the middle of the night, the innkeeper quarrelled so violently with his wife that we all leant out into the courtyard to look, and saw the vines laced about among the pillars and the stars white in the sky. The moment was stabilized, stamped like a coin indelibly among a million that slipped by imperceptibly. There, too, was the melancholy Englishman, who rose among the coffee cups and the little iron tables and revealed the secrets of his soul--as travellers do. All this--Italy, the windy morning, the vines laced about the pillars, the Englishman and the secrets of his soul--rise up in a cloud from the china bowl on the mantelpiece. And there, as our eyes fall to the floor, is that brown stain on the carpet. Mr. Lloyd George made that. "The man's a devil!" said Mr. Cummings, putting the kettle down with which he was about to fill the teapot so that it burnt a brown ring on the carpet.

But when the door shuts on us, all that vanishes. The shell-like covering which our souls have excreted to house themselves, to make for themselves a shape distinct from others, is broken, and there is left of all these wrinkles and roughnesses a central oyster of perceptiveness, an enormous eye. How beautiful a street is in winter! It is at once revealed and obscured. Here vaguely one can trace symmetrical straight avenues of doors and windows; here under the lamps are floating islands of pale light through which pass quickly bright men and women, who, for all their poverty and shabbiness, wear a certain look of unreality, an air of triumph, as if they had given life the slip, so that life, deceived of her prey, blunders on without them. But, after all, we are only gliding smoothly on the surface. The eye is not a miner, not a diver, not a seeker after buried treasure. It floats us smoothly down a stream; resting, pausing, the brain sleeps perhaps as it looks.

How beautiful a London street is then, with its islands of light, and its long groves of darkness, and on one side of it perhaps some tree-sprinkled, grass-grown space where night is folding herself to sleep naturally and, as one passes the iron railing, one hears those little cracklings and stirrings of leaf and twig which seem to suppose the silence of fields all round them, an owl hooting, and far away the rattle of a train in the valley. But this is London, we are reminded; high among the bare trees are hung oblong frames of reddish yellow light--windows; there are points of brilliance burning steadily like low stars--lamps; this empty ground, which holds the country in it and its peace, is only a London square, set about by offices and houses where at this hour fierce lights burn over maps, over documents, over desks where clerks sit turning with wetted forefinger the files of endless correspondences; or more suffusedly the firelight wavers and the lamplight falls upon the privacy of some drawing-room, its easy chairs, its papers, its china, its inlaid table, and the figure of a woman, accurately measuring out the precise number of spoons of tea which----She looks at the door as if she heard a ring downstairs and somebody asking, is she in?

But here we must stop peremptorily. We are in danger of digging deeper than the eye approves; we are impeding our passage down the smooth stream by catching at some branch or root. At any moment, the sleeping army may stir itself and wake in us a thousand violins and trumpets in response; the army of human beings may rouse itself and assert all its oddities and sufferings and sordidities. Let us dally a little longer, be content still with surfaces only--the glossy brilliance of the motor omnibuses; the carnal splendour of the butchers' shops with their yellow flanks and purple steaks; the blue and red bunches of flowers burning so bravely through the plate glass of the florists' windows.

For the eye has this strange property: it rests only on beauty; like a butterfly it seeks colour and basks in warmth. On a winter's night like this, when nature has been at pains to polish and preen herself, it brings back the prettiest trophies, breaks off little lumps of emerald and coral as if the whole earth were made of precious stone. The thing it cannot do (one is speaking of the average unprofessional eye) is to compose these trophies in such a way as to bring out the more obscure angles and relationships. Hence after a prolonged diet of this simple, sugary fare, of beauty pure and uncomposed, we become conscious of satiety. We halt at the door of the boot shop and make some little excuse, which has nothing to do with the real reason, for folding up the bright paraphernalia of the streets and withdrawing to some duskier chamber of the being where we may ask, as we raise our left foot obediently upon the stand: "What, then, is it like to be a dwarf?"

She came in escorted by two women who, being of normal size, looked like benevolent giants beside her. Smiling at the shop girls, they seemed to be disclaiming any lot in her deformity and assuring her of their protection. She wore the peevish yet apologetic expression usual on the faces of the deformed. She needed their kindness, yet she resented it. But when the shop girl had been summoned and the giantesses, smiling indulgently, had asked for shoes for "this lady" and the girl had pushed the little stand in front of her, the dwarf stuck her foot out with an impetuosity which seemed to claim all our attention. Look at that! Look at that! she seemed to demand of us all, as she thrust her foot out, for behold it was the shapely, perfectly proportioned foot of a well-grown woman. It was arched; it was aristocratic. Her whole manner changed as she looked at it resting on the stand. She looked soothed and satisfied. Her manner became full of self-confidence. She sent for shoe after shoe; she tried on pair after pair. She got up and pirouetted before a glass which reflected the foot only in yellow shoes, in fawn shoes, in shoes of lizard skin. She raised her little skirts and displayed her little legs. She was thinking that, after all, feet

61

are the most important part of the whole person; women, she said to herself, have been loved for their feet alone. Seeing nothing but her feet, she imagined perhaps that the rest of her body was of a piece with those beautiful feet. She was shabbily dressed, but she was ready to lavish any money upon her shoes. And as this was the only occasion upon which she was hot afraid of being looked at but positively craved attention, she was ready to use any device to prolong the choosing and fitting. Look at my feet, she seemed to be saying, as she took a step this way and then a step that way. The shop girl good-humouredly must have said something flattering, for suddenly her face lit up in ecstasy. But, after all, the giantesses, benevolent though they were, had their own affairs to see to; she must make up her mind; she must decide which to choose. At length, the pair was chosen and, as she walked out between her guardians, with the parcel swinging from her finger, the ecstasy faded, knowledge returned, the old peevishness, the old apology came back, and by the time she had reached the street again she had become a dwarf only.

But she had changed the mood; she had called into being an atmosphere which, as we followed her out into the street, seemed actually to create the humped, the twisted, the deformed. Two bearded men, brothers, apparently, stone-blind, supporting themselves by resting a hand on the head of a small boy between them, marched down the street. On they came with the unyielding yet tremulous tread of the blind, which seems to lend to their approach something of the terror and inevitability of the fate that has overtaken them. As they passed, holding straight on, the little convoy seemed to cleave asunder the passers-by with the momentum of its silence, its directness, its disaster. Indeed, the dwarf had started a hobbling grotesque dance to which everybody in the street now conformed: the stout lady tightly swathed in shiny sealskin; the feeble-minded boy sucking the silver knob of his stick; the old man squatted on a doorstep as if, suddenly overcome by the absurdity of the human spectacle, he had sat down to look at it--all joined in the hobble and tap of the dwarf's dance.

In what crevices and crannies, one might ask, did they lodge, this maimed company of the halt and the blind? Here, perhaps, in the top rooms of these narrow old houses between Holborn and Soho, where people have such queer names, and pursue so many curious trades, are gold beaters, accordion pleaters, cover buttons, or support life, with even greater fantasticality, upon a traffic in cups without saucers, china umbrella handles, and highly-coloured pictures of martyred saints. There they lodge, and it seems as if the lady in the sealskin jacket must find life tolerable, passing the time of day with the accordion pleater, or the man who covers buttons; life which is so fantastic cannot be altogether tragic. They do not grudge us, we are musing, our prosperity; when, suddenly, turning the corner, we come upon a bearded Jew, wild, hunger-bitten, glaring out of his misery; or pass the humped body of an old woman flung abandoned on the step of a public building with a cloak over her like the hasty

63

covering thrown over a dead horse or donkey. At such sights the nerves of the spine seem to stand erect; a sudden flare is brandished in our eyes; a question is asked which is never answered. Often enough these derelicts choose to lie not a stone's thrown from theatres, within hearing of barrel organs, almost, as night draws on, within touch of the sequined cloaks and bright legs of diners and dancers. They lie close to those shop windows where commerce offers to a world of old women laid on doorsteps, of blind men, of hobbling dwarfs, sofas which are supported by the gilt necks of proud swans; tables inlaid with baskets of many coloured fruit; sideboards paved with green marble the better to support the weight of boars' heads; and carpets so softened with age that their carnations have almost vanished in a pale green sea.

Passing, glimpsing, everything seems accidentally but miraculously sprinkled with beauty, as if the tide of trade which deposits its burden so punctually and prosaically upon the shores of Oxford Street had this night cast up nothing but treasure. With no thought of buying, the eye is sportive and generous; it creates; it adorns; it enhances. Standing out in the street, one may build up all the chambers of an imaginary house and furnish them at one's will with sofa, table, carpet. That rug will do for the hall. That alabaster bowl shall stand on a carved table in the window. Our merrymaking shall be reflected in that thick round mirror. But, having built and furnished the house, one is happily under no obligation to possess it; one can dismantle it in the twinkling of an eye, and build and furnish another house with other chairs and other glasses. Or let us indulge ourselves at the antique jewellers, among the trays of rings and the hanging necklaces. Let us choose those pearls, for example, and then imagine how, if we put them on, life would be changed. It becomes instantly between two and three in the morning; the lamps are burning very white in the deserted streets of Mayfair. Only motor-cars are abroad at this hour, and one has a sense of emptiness, of airiness, of secluded gaiety. Wearing pearls, wearing silk, one steps out on to a balcony which overlooks the gardens of sleeping Mayfair. There are a few lights in the bedrooms of great peers returned from Court, of silk-stockinged footmen, of dowagers who have pressed the hands of statesmen. A cat creeps along the garden wall. Love-making is going on sibilantly, seductively in the darker places of the room behind thick green curtains. Strolling sedately as if he were promenading a terrace beneath which the shires and counties of England lie sun-bathed, the aged Prime Minister recounts to Lady So-and-So with the curls and the emeralds the true history of some great crisis in the affairs of the land. We seem to be riding on the top of the highest mast of the tallest ship; and yet at the same time we know that nothing of this sort matters; love is not proved thus, nor great achievements completed thus; so that we sport with the moment and preen our feathers in it lightly, as we stand on the balcony watching the moonlit cat creep along Princess Mary's garden wall.

But what could be more absurd? It is, in fact, on the stroke of six; it is a winter's evening; we are walking to the Strand to buy a pencil. How, then, are we also on a balcony, wearing pearls in June? What could be more absurd? Yet it is nature's folly, not ours. When she set about her chief masterpiece, the making of man, she should have thought of one thing only. Instead, turning her head, looking over her shoulder, into each one of us she let creep instincts and desires which are utterly at variance with his main being, so that we are streaked, variegated, all of a mixture; the colours have run. Is the true self this which stands on the pavement in January, or that which bends over the balcony in June? Am I here, or am I there? Or is the true self neither this nor that, neither here nor there, but something so varied and wandering that it is only when we give the rein to its wishes and let it take its way unimpeded that we are indeed ourselves? Circumstances compel unity; for convenience sake a man must be a whole. The good citizen when he opens his door in the evening must be banker, golfer, husband, father; not a nomad wandering the desert, a mystic staring at the sky, a debauchee in the slums of San Francisco, a soldier heading a revolution, a pariah howling with scepticism and solitude. When he opens his door, he must run his fingers through his hair and put his umbrella in the stand like the rest.

But here, none too soon, are the second-hand bookshops. Here we find anchorage in these thwarting currents of being; here we balance ourselves after the splendours and miseries of the streets. The very sight of the bookseller's wife with her foot on the fender, sitting beside a good coal fire, screened from the door, is sobering and cheerful. She is never reading, or only the newspaper; her talk, when it leaves bookselling, which it does so gladly, is about hats; she likes a hat to be practical, she says, as well as pretty. O no, they don't live at the shop; they live in Brixton; she must have a bit of green to look at. In summer a jar of flowers grown in her own garden is stood on the top of some dusty pile to enliven the shop. Books are everywhere; and always the same sense of adventure fills us. Second-hand books are wild books, homeless books; they have come together in vast flocks of variegated feather, and have a charm which the domesticated volumes of the library lack. Besides, in this random miscellaneous company we may rub against some complete stranger who will, with luck, turn into the best friend we have in the world. There is always a hope, as we reach down some grayish-white book from an upper shelf, directed by its air of shabbiness and desertion, of meeting here with a man who set out on horseback over a hundred years ago to explore the woollen market in the Midlands and Wales; an unknown traveller, who stayed at inns, drank his pint, noted pretty girls and serious customs, wrote it all down stiffly, laboriously for sheer love of it (the book was published at his own expense); was infinitely prosy, busy, and matter-of-fact, and so let flow in without his knowing it the very scent of hollyhocks and the hay together with such a portrait of himself as gives him forever a seat in the warm corner of the mind's inglenook. One may buy him for eighteen pence now. He is marked three and sixpence, but the bookseller's wife, seeing how shabby the covers are and how long the book has stood there since it was bought at some sale of a gentleman's library in Suffolk, will let it go at that.

Thus, glancing round the bookshop, we make other such sudden capricious friendships with the unknown and the vanished whose only record is, for example, this little book of poems, so fairly printed, so finely engraved, too, with a portrait of the author. For he was a poet and drowned untimely, and his verse, mild as it is and formal and sententious, sends forth still a frail fluty sound like that of a piano organ played in some back street resignedly by an old Italian organ-grinder in a corduroy jacket. There are travellers, too, row upon row of them, still testifying, indomitable spinsters that they were, to the discomforts that they endured and the sunsets they admired in Greece when Queen Victoria was a girl. A tour in Cornwall with a visit to the tin mines was thought worthy of voluminous record. People went slowly up the Rhine and did portraits of each other in Indian ink, sitting reading on deck beside a coil of rope; they measured the pyramids; were lost to civilization for years; converted negroes in pestilential swamps. This packing up and going off, exploring deserts and catching fevers, settling in India for a lifetime, penetrating even to China and then returning to lead a parochial life at Edmonton, tumbles and tosses upon the dusty floor like an uneasy sea, so restless the English are, with the waves at their very door. The waters of travel and adventure seem to break upon little islands of serious effort and lifelong industry stood in jagged column upon the floor. In these piles of puce-bound volumes with gilt monograms on the back, thoughtful clergymen expound the gospels; scholars are to be heard with their hammers and their chisels chipping clear the ancient texts of Euripides and Aeschylus. Thinking, annotating, expounding goes on at a prodigious rate all around us and over everything, like a punctual, everlasting tide, washes the ancient sea of fiction. Innumerable volumes tell how Arthur loved Laura and they were separated and they were unhappy and then they met and they were happy ever after, as was the way when Victoria ruled these islands.

The number of books in the world is infinite, and one is forced to glimpse and nod and move on after a moment of talk, a flash of understanding, as, in the street outside, one catches a word in passing and from a chance phrase fabricates a lifetime. It is about a woman called Kate that they are talking, how "I said to her quite straight last night . . . if you don't think I'm worth a penny stamp, I said . . ." But who Kate is, and to what crisis in their friendship that penny stamp refers, we shall never know; for Kate sinks under the warmth of their volubility; and here, at the street corner, another page of the volume of life is laid open by the sight of two men consulting under the lamp-post. They are spelling out the latest wire from Newmarket in the stop press news. Do they think, then, that fortune will ever convert their rags into fur and broadcloth, sling them with watch-chains, and plant diamond pins where there is now a ragged open shirt? But the main stream of walkers at this hour sweeps too fast to let us ask such questions. They are wrapt, in this short passage from work to home, in some narcotic dream, now that they are free from the desk, and have the fresh air on their cheeks.

They put on those bright clothes which they must hang up and lock the key upon all the rest of the day, and are great cricketers, famous actresses, soldiers who have saved their country at the hour of need. Dreaming, gesticulating, often muttering a few words aloud, they sweep over the Strand and across Waterloo Bridge whence they will be slung in long rattling trains, to some prim little villa in Barnes or Surbiton where the sight of the clock in the hall and the smell of the supper in the basement puncture the dream.

But we are come to the Strand now, and as we hesitate on the curb, a little rod about the length of one's finger begins to lay its bar across the velocity and abundance of life. "Really I must--really I must"--that is it. Without investigating the demand, the mind cringes to the accustomed tyrant. One must, one always must, do something or other; it is not allowed one simply to enjoy oneself. Was it not for this reason that, some time ago, we fabricated the excuse, and invented the necessity of buying something? But what was it? Ah, we remember, it was a pencil. Let us go then and buy this pencil. But just as we are turning to obey the command, another self disputes the right of the tyrant to insist. The usual conflict comes about. Spread out behind the rod of duty we see the whole breadth of the river Thames--wide, mournful, peaceful. And we see it through the eyes of somebody who is leaning over the Embankment on a summer evening, without a care in the world. Let us put off buying the pencil; let us go in search of this person--and soon it becomes apparent that this person is ourselves. For if we could stand there where we stood six months ago, should we not be again as we were then--calm, aloof, content? Let us try then. But the river is rougher and greyer than we remembered. The tide is running out to sea. It brings down with it a tug and two barges, whose load of straw is tightly bound down beneath tarpaulin covers. There is, too, close by us, a couple leaning over the balustrade with the curious lack of self-consciousness lovers have, as if the importance of the affair they are engaged on claims without question the indulgence of the human race. The sights we see and the sounds we hear now have none of the quality of the past; nor have we any share in the serenity of the person who, six months ago, stood precisely were we stand now. His is the happiness of death; ours the insecurity of life. He has no future; the future is even now invading our peace. It is only when we look at the past and take from it the element of uncertainty that we can enjoy perfect peace. As it is, we must turn, we must cross the Strand again, we must find a shop where, even at this hour, they will be ready to sell us a pencil.

It is always an adventure to enter a new room for the lives and characters of its owners have distilled their atmosphere into it, and directly we enter it we breast some new wave of emotion. Here, without a doubt, in the stationer's shop people had been quarrelling. Their anger shot through the air. They both stopped; the old woman--they were husband and wife evidently--retired to a back room; the old man whose rounded forehead and globular eyes would have looked well on the frontispiece of some Elizabethan folio, stayed to serve us. "A pencil, a pencil," he repeated, "certainly, certainly." He spoke with the distraction yet effusiveness of one whose emotions have been roused and checked in full flood. He began opening box after box and shutting them again. He said that it was very difficult to find things when they kept so many different articles. He launched into a story about some legal gentleman who had got into deep waters owing to the conduct of his wife. He had known him for years; he had been connected with the Temple for half a century, he said, as if he wished his wife in the back room to overhear him. He upset a box of rubber bands. At last, exasperated by his incompetence, he pushed the swing door open and called out roughly: "Where d'you keep the pencils?" as if his wife had hidden them. The old lady came in. Looking at nobody, she put her hand with a fine air of righteous severity upon the right box. There were pencils. How then could he do without her? Was she not indispensable to him? In order to keep them there, standing side by side in forced neutrality, one had to be particular in one's choice of pencils; this was too soft, that too hard. They stood silently looking on. The longer they stood there, the calmer they grew; their heat was going down, their anger disappearing. Now, without a word said on either side, the quarrel was made up. The old man, who would not have disgraced Ben Jonson's title-page, reached the box back to its proper place, bowed profoundly his good-night to us, and they disappeared. She would get out her sewing; he would read his newspaper; the canary would scatter them impartially with seed. The quarrel was over.

In these minutes in which a ghost has been sought for, a quarrel composed, and a pencil bought, the streets had become completely empty. Life had withdrawn to the top floor, and lamps were lit. The pavement was dry and hard; the road was of hammered silver. Walking home through the desolation one could tell oneself the story of the dwarf, of the blind men, of the party in the Mayfair mansion, of the quarrel in the stationer's shop. Into each of these lives one could penetrate a little way, far enough to give oneself the illusion that one is not tethered to a single mind, but can put on briefly for a few minutes the bodies and minds of others. One could become a washerwoman, a publican, a street singer. And what greater delight and wonder can there be than to leave the straight lines of personality and deviate into those footpaths that lead beneath brambles and thick tree trunks into the heart of the forest where live those wild beasts, our fellow men?

That is true: to escape is the greatest of pleasures; street haunting in winter the greatest of adventures. Still as we approach our own doorstep again, it is comforting to feel the old possessions, the old prejudices, fold us round; and the self, which has been blown about at so many street corners, which has battered like a moth at the flame of so many inaccessible lanterns, sheltered and enclosed. Here again is the usual door; here the chair turned as we left it and the china bowl and the brown ring on the carpet. And here--let us examine it tenderly, let us touch it with reverence--is the only spoil we have retrieved from all the treasures of the city, a lead pencil.

JONES AND WILKINSON(Drawn from the MEMOIRS OF TATE WILKINSON,4 vols.,1790.)

Whether Jones should come before Wilkinson or Wilkinson before Jones is not a matter likely to agitate many breasts at the present moment, seeing that more than a hundred and fifty years have rolled over the gentlemen in question and diminished a lustre which, even in their own time, round about the year 1750, was not very bright. The Rev. Dr. Wilkinson might indeed claim precedence by virtue of his office. He was His Majesty's Chaplain of the Savoy and Chaplain also to his late Royal Highness, Frederick Prince of Wales. But then Dr. Wilkinson was transported. Captain James Jones might assert that, as Captain of His Majesty's third regiment of Guards with a residence by virtue of his office in Savoy Square, his social position was equal to the Doctor's. But Captain Jones had to seclude himself beyond the reach of the law at Mortlake. What, however, renders these comparisons peculiarly odious is the fact that the Captain and the Doctor were boon companions whose tastes were congenial, whose incomes were insufficient, whose wives drank tea together, and whose houses in the Savoy were not two hundred yards apart. Dr. Wilkinson, for all his sacred offices (he was Rector of Coyty in Glamorgan, stipendiary curate of Wise in Kent, and, through Lord Galway, had the right to "open plaister-pits in the honour of Pontefract"), was a convivial spirit who cut a splendid figure in the pulpit, preached and read prayers in a voice that was clear, strong and sonorous so that many a lady of fashion never "missed her pew near the pulpit," and persons of title remembered him many years after misfortune had removed the handsome preacher from their sight.

Captain Jones shared many of his friend's qualities. He was vivacious, witty, and generous, well made and elegant in person and, if he was not quite as handsome as the doctor, he was perhaps rather his superior in intellect. Compare them as we may, however, there can be little doubt that the gifts and tastes of both gentlemen were better adapted for pleasure than for labour, for society than for solitude, for the hazards and pleasures of the table rather than for the rigours of religion and war. It was the gaming-table that seduced Captain Jones, and here, alas, his gifts and graces stood him in little stead. His affairs became more and more hopelessly embarrassed, so that shortly, instead of being able to take his walks at large, he was forced to limit them to the precincts of St. James's, where, by ancient prerogative, such unfortunates as he were free from the attentions of the bailiffs.

To so gregarious a spirit the confinement was irksome. His only resource, indeed, was to get into talk with any such "parksaunterers" as misfortunes like his own had driven to perambulate the Park, or, when the weather allowed, to bask and loiter and gossip on its benches. As chance would have it (and the Captain was a devotee of that goddess) he found himself one day resting on the same bench with an elderly gentleman of military aspect and stern demeanour, whose ill-temper the wit and humour which all allowed to Captain

Jones presumably beguiled, so that whenever the Captain appeared in the Park, the old man sought his company, and they passed the time until dinner very pleasantly in talk. On no occasion, however, did the General--for it appeared that the name of this morose old man was General Skelton--ask Captain Jones to his house; the acquaintance went no further than the bench in St. James's Park; and when, as soon fell out, the Captain's difficulties forced him to the greater privacy of a little cabin at Mortlake, he forgot entirely the military gentleman who, presumably, still sought an appetite for dinner or some alleviation of his own sour mood in loitering and gossiping with the park-saunterers of St. James's.

But among the amiable characteristics of Captain Jones was a love of wife and child, scarcely to be wondered at, indeed, considering his wife's lively and entertaining disposition and the extraordinary promise of that little girl who was later to become the wife of Lord Cornwallis. At whatever risk to himself, Captain Jones would steal back to revisit his wife and to hear his little girl recite the part of Juliet which, under his teaching, she had perfectly by heart. On one such secret journey he was hurrying to get within the royal sanctuary of St. James's when a voice called on him to stop. His fears obsessing him, he hurried the faster, his pursuer close at his heels. Realizing that escape was impossible, Jones wheeled about and facing his pursuer, whom he recognized as the Attorney Brown, demanded what his enemy wanted of him. Far from being his enemy, said Brown, he was the best friend he had ever had, which he would prove if Jones would accompany him to the first tavern that came to hand. There, in a private room over a fire, Mr. Brown disclosed the following astonishing story. An unknown friend, he said, who had scrutinized Jones's conduct carefully and concluded that his deserts outweighed his misdemeanours, was prepared to settle all his debts and indeed to put him beyond the reach of such tormentors in future. At these words a load was lifted from Jones's heart, and he cried out "Good God! Who can this paragon of friendship be?" It was none other, said Brown, than General Skelton. General Skelton, the man whom he had only met to chat with on a bench in St. James's Park? Jones asked in wonderment. Yes, it was the General, Brown assured him. Then let him hasten to throw himself in gratitude at his benefactor's knee! Not so fast, Brown replied; General Skelton will never speak to you again. General Skelton died last night.

The extent of Captain Jones's good fortune was indeed magnificent. The General had left Captain Jones sole heir to all his possessions on no other condition than that he should assume the name of Skelton instead of Jones. Hastening through streets no longer dreadful, since every debt of honour could now be paid, Captain Jones brought his wife the astonishing news of their good fortune, and they promptly set out to view that part which lay nearest to hand--the General's great house in Henrietta Street. Gazing about her, half in dream, half in earnest, Mrs. Jones Was so overcome with the tumult of her emotions that she could not stay to gather in the extent of her possessions, but ran to

Little Bedford Street, where Mrs. Wilkinson was then living, to impart her joy. Meanwhile, the news that General Skelton lay dead in Henrietta Street without a son to succeed him spread abroad, and those who thought themselves his heirs arrived in the house of death to take stock of their inheritance, among them one great and beautiful lady whose avarice was her undoing, whose misfortunes were equal to her sins, Kitty Chudleigh, Countess of Bristol, Duchess of Kingston. Miss Chudleigh, as she then called herself, believed, and who can doubt that with her passionate nature, her lust for wealth and property, her pistols and her parsimony, she believed with vehemence and asserted her belief with arrogance, that all General Skelton's property had legally descended to her. Later, when the will was read and the truth made public that not only the house in Henrietta Street, but Pap Castle in Cumberland and the lands and lead mines pertaining to it, were left without exception to an unknown Captain Jones, she burst out in "terms exceeding all bounds of delicacy." She cried that her relative the General was an old fool in his dotage, that Jones and his wife were impudent low upstarts beneath her notice, and so flounced into her coach "with a scornful quality toss" to carry on that life of deceit and intrigue and ambition which drove her later to wander in ignominy, an outcast from her country.

What remains to be told of the fortunes of Captain Jones can be briefly despatched. Having new furnished the house in Henrietta Street, the Jones family set out when summer came to visit their estates in Cumberland. The country was so fair, the Castle so stately, the thought that now all belonged to them so gratifying that their progress for three weeks was one of unmixed pleasure and the spot where they were now to live seemed a paradise. But there was an eagerness, an impetuosity about James Jones which made him impatient to suffer even the smiles of fortune passively. He must be active--he must be up and doing. He must be "let down," for all his friends could do to dissuade him, to view a lead mine. The consequences as they foretold were disastrous. He was drawn up, indeed, but already infected with a deadly sickness of which in a few days he died, in the arms of his wife, in the midst of that paradise which he had toiled so long to reach and now was to die without enjoying.

Meanwhile the Wilkinsons--but that name, alas, was no longer applicable to them, nor did the Dr. and his wife any more inhabit the house in the Savoy--the Wilkinsons had suffered more extremities at the hands of Fate than the Joneses themselves. Dr. Wilkinson, it has been said, resembled his friend Jones in the conviviality of his habits and his inability to keep within the limits of his income. Indeed, his wife's dowry of two thousand pounds had gone to pay off the debts of his youth. But by what means could he pay off the debts of his middle age? He was now past fifty, and what with good company and good living, was seldom free from duns, and always pressed for money. Suddenly, from an unexpected quarter, help appeared. This was none other than the Marriage Act, passed in 1755, which laid it down that if any person solemnized a marriage without publishing the banns, unless a marriage licence had already been obtained, he should be subject to transportation for fourteen years. Dr. Wilkinson, looking at the matter, it is to be feared, from his own angle, and with a view to his own necessities, argued that as Chaplain of the Savoy, which was extra-Parochial and Royal-exempt, he could grant licences as usual--a privilege which at once brought him such a glut of business, such a crowd of couples wishing to be married in a hurry, that the rat-tat-tat never ceased on his street door, and cash flooded the family exchequer so that even his little boy's pockets were lined with gold. The duns were paid; the table sumptuously spread. But Dr. Wilkinson shared another failing with his friend Jones; he would not take advice. His friends warned him; the Government plainly hinted that if he persisted they would be forced to act. Secure in what he imagined to be his right, enjoying the prosperity it brought him to the full, the Doctor paid no heed. On Easter Day he was engaged in marrying from eight in the morning till twelve at night. At last, one Sunday, the King's Messengers appeared. The Doctor escaped by a secret walk over the leads of the Savoy, made his way to the river bank, where he slipped upon some logs and fell, heavy and elderly as he was, in the mud; but nevertheless got to Somerset stairs, took a boat, and reached the Kentish shore in safety. Even now he brazened it out that the law was on his side, and came back four weeks later prepared to stand his trial. Once more, for the last time, company overflowed the house in the Savoy; lawyers abounded, and, as they ate and drank, assured Dr. Wilkinson that his case was already won. In July 1756 the trial began. But what conclusion could there be? The crime had been committed and persisted in openly in spite of warning. The Doctor was found guilty and sentenced to fourteen years' transportation.

It remained for his friends to fit him out, like the gentleman he was, for his voyage to America. There, they argued, his gifts of speech and person would make him welcome, and later his wife and son could join him. To them he bade farewell in the dismal precincts of Newgate in March 1757. But contrary winds beat the ship back to shore; the gout seized on a body enfeebled by pleasure and adversity; at Plymouth Dr. Wilkinson was transported finally and for ever. The lead mine undid Jones; the Marriage Act was the downfall of Wilkinson. Both now sleep in peace, Jones in Cumberland, Wilkinson, far from his friend (and if their failings were great, great too were their gifts and graces) on the shores of the melancholy Atlantic.

"TWELFTH NIGHT" AT THE OLD VIC (* Written in 1933.)

Shakespeareans are divided, it is well known, into three classes; those who prefer to read Shakespeare in the book; those who prefer to see him acted on the stage; and those who run perpetually from book to stage gathering plunder. Certainly there is a good deal to be said for reading TWELFTH NIGHT in the book if the book can be read in a garden, with no sound but the thud of an apple falling to the earth, or of the wind ruffling the branches of the trees. For one thing there is time--time not only to hear "the sweet sound that breathes upon a bank of violets" but to unfold the implications of that very subtle speech as the Duke winds into the nature of love. There is time, too, to make a note in the margin; time to wonder at queer jingles like "that live in her; when liver, brain, and heart" . . . "and of a foolish knight that you brought in one night" and to ask oneself whether it was from them that was born the lovely, "And what should I do in Illyria? My brother he is in Elysium." For Shakespeare is writing, it seems, not with the whole of his mind mobilized and under control but with feelers left flying that sort and play with words so that the trail of a chance word is caught and followed recklessly. From the echo of one word is born another word, for which reason, perhaps, the play seems as we read it to tremble perpetually on the brink of music. They are always calling for songs in TWELFTH NIGHT, "0 fellow come, the song we had last night." Yet

Shakespeare was not so deeply in love with words but that he could turn and laugh at them. "They that do dally with words do quickly make them wanton." There is a roar of laughter and out burst Sir Toby, Sir Andrew, Maria. Words on their lips are things that have meaning; that rush and leap out with a whole character packed in a little phrase. When Sir Andrew says "I was adored once," we feel that we hold him in the hollow of our hands; a novelist would have taken three volumes to bring us to that pitch of intimacy. And Viola, Malvolio, Olivia, the Duke--the mind so brims and spills over with all that we know and guess about them as they move in and out among the lights and shadows of the mind's stage that we ask why should we imprison them within the bodies of real men and women? Why exchange this garden for the theatre? The answer is that Shakespeare wrote for the stage and presumably with reason. Since they are acting TWELFTH NIGHT at the Old Vic, let us compare the two versions.

Many apples might fall without being heard in the Waterloo Road, and as for the shadows, the electric light has consumed them all. The first impression upon entering the Old Vic is overwhelmingly positive and definite. We seem to have issued out from the shadows of the garden upon the bridge of the Parthenon. The metaphor is mixed, but then so is the scenery. The columns of the bridge somehow suggest an Atlantic liner and the austere splendours of a classical temple in combination. But the body is almost as upsetting as the scenery. The actual persons of Malvolio, Sir Toby,

Olivia and the rest expand our visionary characters out of all recognition. At first we are inclined to resent it. You are not Malvolio; or Sir Toby either, we want to tell them; but merely impostors. We sit gaping at the ruins of the play, at the travesty of the play. And then by degrees this same body or rather all these bodies together, take our play and remodel it between them. The play gains immensely in robustness, in solidity. The printed word is changed out of all recognition when it is heard by other people. We watch it strike upon this man or woman; we see them laugh or shrug their shoulders, or turn aside to hide their faces. The word is given a body as well as a soul. Then again as the actors pause, or topple over a barrel, or stretch their hands out, the flatness of the print is broken up as by crevasses or precipices; all the proportions are changed. Perhaps the most impressive effect in the play is achieved by the long pause which Sebastian and Viola make as they stand looking at each other in a silent ecstasy of recognition. The reader's eye may have slipped over that moment entirely. Here we are made to pause and think about it; and are reminded that Shakespeare wrote for the body and for the mind simultaneously.

But now that the actors have done their proper work of solidifying and intensifying our impressions, we begin to criticize them more minutely and to compare their version with our own. We make Mr. Quartermaine's Malvolio stand beside our Malvolio. And to tell the truth, wherever the fault may lie, they have very little in common. Mr. Quartermaine's Malvolio is a splendid gentleman, courteous, considerate, well bred; a man of parts and humour who has no quarrel with the world. He has never felt a twinge of vanity or a moment's envy in his life. If Sir Toby and Maria fool him he sees through it, we may be sure, and only suffers it as a fine gentleman puts up with the games of foolish children. Our Malvolio, on the other hand, was a fantastic complex creature, twitching with vanity, tortured by ambition. There was cruelty in his teasing, and a hint of tragedy in his defeat; his final threat had a momentary terror in it. But when Mr. Quartermaine says "I'll be revenged on the whole pack of you," we feel merely that the powers of the law will be soon and effectively invoked. What, then, becomes of Olivia's "He hath been most notoriously abused"? Then there is Olivia. Madame Lopokova has by nature that rare quality which is neither to be had for the asking nor to be subdued by the will--the genius of personality. She has only to float on to the stage and everything round her suffers, not a sea change, but a change into light, into gaiety; the birds sing, the sheep are garlanded, the air rings with melody and human beings dance towards each other on the tips of their toes possessed of an exquisite friendliness, sympathy and delight. But our Olivia was a stately lady; of sombre complexion, slow moving, and of few sympathies. She could not love the Duke nor change her feeling. Madame Lopokova loves everybody. She is always changing. Her hands, her face, her feet, the whole of her body, are always quivering in sympathy with the moment. She could make the moment, as she proved when she walked down the stairs with Sebastian, one of intense and moving beauty; but she was not our Olivia. Compared with her the comic group, Sir Toby, Sir Andrew, Maria, the fool were more than ordinarily English. Coarse, humorous, robust, they trolled out their words, they rolled over their barrels; they acted magnificently. No reader, one may make bold to say, could outpace Miss Seyler's Maria, with its quickness, its inventiveness, its merriment; nor add anything to the humours of Mr. Livesey's Sir Toby. And Miss Jeans as Viola was satisfactory; and Mr. Hare as Antonio was admirable; and Mr. Morland's clown was a good clown. What, then, was lacking in the play as a whole? Perhaps that it was not a whole. The fault may lie partly with Shakespeare. It is easier to act his comedy than his poetry, one may suppose, for when he wrote as a poet he was apt to write too quick for the human tongue. The prodigality of his metaphors can be flashed over by the eye, but the speaking voice falters in the middle. Hence the comedy was out of proportion to the rest. Then, perhaps, the actors were too highly charged with individuality or too incongruously cast. They broke the play up into separate pieces--now we were in the groves of Arcady, now in some inn at Blackfriars. The mind in reading spins a web from scene to scene, compounds a background from apples falling, and the toll of a church bell, and an owl's fantastic flight which keeps the play together. Here that continuity was sacrificed. We left the theatre possessed of many brilliant fragments but without the sense of all things conspiring and combining together which may be the satisfying culmination of a less brilliant performance.

Nevertheless, the play has served its purpose. It has made us compare our Malvolio with Mr. Quartermaine's; our Olivia with Madame Lopokova's; our reading of the whole play with Mr. Guthrie's; and since they all differ back we must go to Shakespeare. We must read TWELFTH NIGHT again. Mr. Guthrie has made that necessary and whetted our appetite for the CHERRY ORCHARD, MEASURE FOR MEASURE, and HENRY THE EIGHTH that are still to come.

MADAME DE SÉVIGNÉ

This great lady, this robust and fertile letter writer, who in our age would probably have been one of the great novelists, takes up presumably as much space in the consciousness of living readers as any figure of her vanished age. But it is more difficult to fix that figure within an outline than so to sum up many of her contemporaries. That is partly because she created her being, not in plays or poems, but in letters--touch by touch, with repetitions, amassing daily trifles, writing down what came into her head as if she were talking. Thus the fourteen volumes of her letters enclose a vast open space, like one of her own great woods; the rides are crisscrossed with the intricate shadows of branches, figures roam down the glades, pass from sun to shadow, are lost to sight, appear again, but never sit down in fixed attitudes to compose a group.

Thus we live in her presence, and often fall, as with living people, into unconsciousness. She goes on talking, we half listen. And then something she says rouses us. We add it to her character, so that the character grows and changes, and she seems like a living person, inexhaustible.

This of course is one of the qualities that all letter writers possess, and she, because of her unconscious naturalness, her flow and abundance, possesses it far more than the brilliant Walpole, for example, or the reserved and self-conscious Gray. Perhaps in the long run we know her more instinctively, more profoundly, than we know them. We sink deeper down into her, and know by instinct rather than by reason how she will feel; this she will be amused by; that will take her fancy; now she will plunge into melancholy. Her range too is larger than theirs; there is more scope and more diversity. Everything seems to yield its juice--its fun, its enjoyment; or to feed her meditations. She has a robust appetite; nothing shocks her; she gets nourishment from whatever is set before her. She is an intellectual, quick to enjoy the wit of La Rochefoucauld, to relish the fine discrimination of Madame de La Fayette. She has a natural dwelling place in books, so that Josephus or Pascal or the absurd long romances of the time are not read by her so much as embedded in her mind. Their verses, their stories rise to her lips along with her own thoughts. But there is a sensibility in her which intensifies this great appetite for many things. It is of course shown at its most extreme, its most irrational, in her love for her daughter. She loves her as an elderly man loves a young mistress who tortures him. It was a passion that was twisted and morbid; it caused her many humiliations; sometimes it made her ashamed of herself. For, from the daughter's point of view it was exhausting, was embarrassing to be the object of such intense emotion; and she could not always respond. She feared that her mother was making her ridiculous in the eyes of her friends. Also she felt that she was not like that. She was different; colder, more fastidious, less robust. Her mother was ignoring the real daughter in this flood of adoration for a daughter who did not exist. She was forced to curb her; to assert her own identity. It was inevitable that

Madame de Sévigné, with her exacerbated sensibility, should feel hurt.

Sometimes, therefore, Madame de Sévigné weeps. The daughter does not love her. That is a thought so bitter, and a fear so perpetual and so profound, that life loses its savour; she has recourse to sages, to poets to console her; and reflects with sadness upon the vanity of life; and how death will come. Then, too, she is agitated beyond what is right or reasonable, because a letter has not reached her. Then she knows that she has been absurd; and realizes that she is boring her friends with this obsession. What is worse, she has bored her daughter. And then when the bitter drop has fallen, up bubbles quicker and quicker the ebullition of that robust vitality, of that irrepressible quick enjoyment, that natural relish for life, as if she instinctively repaired her failure by fluttering all her feathers; by making every facet glitter. She shakes herself out of her glooms; makes fun of "les D'Hacquevilles"; collects a handful of gossip; the latest news of the King and Madame de Maintenon; how Charles has fallen in love; how the ridiculous Mademoiselle de Plessis has been foolish again; when she wanted a handkerchief to spit into, the silly woman tweaked her nose; or describes how she has been amusing herself by amazing the simple little girl who lives at the end of the park--la petite personne--with stories of kings and countries, of all that great world that she who has lived in the thick of it knows so well. At last, comforted, assured for the time being at least of her daughter's love, she lets herself relax; and throwing off all disguises, tells her daughter how nothing in the world pleases her so well as solitude. She is happiest alone in the country. She loves rambling alone in her woods. She loves going out by herself at night. She loves hiding from callers. She loves walking among her trees and musing. She loves the gardener's chatter; she loves planting. She loves the gipsy girl who dances, as her own daughter used to dance, but not of course so exquisitely.

It is natural to use the present tense, because we live in her presence. We are very little conscious of a disturbing medium between us--that she is living, after all, by means of written words. But now and then with the sound of her voice in our ears and its rhythm rising and falling within us, we become aware, with some sudden phrase, about spring, about a country neighbour, something struck off in a flash, that we are, of course, being addressed by one of the great mistresses of the art of speech.

Then we listen for a time, consciously. How, we wonder, does she contrive to make us follow every word of the story of the cook who killed himself because the fish failed to come in time for the royal dinner party; or the scene of the haymaking; or the anecdote of the servant whom she dismissed in a sudden rage; how does she achieve this order, this perfection of composition? Did she practise her art? It seems not. Did she tear up and correct? There is no record of any painstaking or effort. She says again and again that she writes her letters as she speaks. She begins one as she sends off another; there is the page on her desk and she fills it, in the intervals of all her other avocations. People are interrupting; servants are coming for orders. She entertains; she is at the beck and call of her friends. It seems then that she must have been so imbued with good sense, by the age she lived in, by the company she kept--La Rochefoucauld's wisdom, Madame de La Fayette's conversation, by hearing now a play by Racine, by reading Montaigne, Rabelais, or Pascal; perhaps by sermons, perhaps by some of those songs that Coulanges was always singing--she must have imbibed so much that was sane and wholesome unconsciously that, when she took up her pen, it followed unconsciously the laws she had learnt by heart. Marie de Rabutin it seems was born into a group where the elements were so richly and happily mixed that it drew out her virtue instead of opposing it. She was helped, not thwarted. Nothing baffled or contracted or withered her. What opposition she encountered was only enough to confirm her judgment. For she was highly conscious of folly, of vice, of pretention. She was a born critic, and a critic whose judgments were inborn, unhesitating. She is always referring her impressions to a standard--hence the incisiveness, the depth and the comedy that make those spontaneous statements so illuminating. There is nothing naive about her. She is by no means a simple spectator. Maxims fall from her pen. She sums up; she judges. But it is done effortlessly. She has inherited the standard and accepts it without effort. She is heir to a tradition, which stands guardian and gives proportion. The gaiety, the colour, the chatter, the many movements of the figures in the foreground have a background. At Les Rochers there is always Paris and the court; at Paris there is Les Rochers, with its solitude, its trees, its peasants. And behind them all again there is virtue, faith, death itself. But this background, while it gives its scale to the moment, is so well established that she is secure. She is free, thus anchored, to explore; to enjoy; to plunge this way and that; to enter wholeheartedly into the myriad humours, pleasures, oddities, and savours of her well nourished, prosperous, delightful present moment.

So she passes with free and stately step from Paris to Brittany from Brittany in her coach and six all across France. She stays with friends on the road; she is attended by a cheerful company of familiars. Wherever she alights she attracts at once the love of some boy or girl; or the exacting admiration of a man of the world like her disagreeable cousin Bussy Rabutin, who cannot rest under her disapproval, but must be assured of her good opinion in spite of all his treachery. The famous and the brilliant also wish to have her company, for she is part of their world; and can take her share in their sophisticated conversations. There is something wise and large and sane about her which draws the confidences of her own son. Feckless and impulsive, the prey of his own weak and charming nature as he is, Charles nurses her with the utmost patience through her rheumatic fever. She laughs at his foibles; knows his failings. She is tolerant and outspoken; nothing need be hidden from her; she knows all that there is to be known of man and his passions.

So she takes her way through the world, and sends her letters, radiant and glowing with all this various traffic from one end of France to the other, twice weekly. As the fourteen volumes so spaciously unfold their story of twenty years it seems that this world is large enough to enclose everything. Here is the garden that Europe has been digging for many centuries; into which so many generations have poured their blood; here it is at last fertilized, bearing flowers. And the flowers are not those rare and solitary blossoms--great men, with their poems, and their conquests. The flowers in this garden are a whole society of full grown men and women from whom want and struggle have been removed; growing together in harmony, each contributing something that the other lacks. By way of proving it, the letters of Madame de Sévigné are often shared by other pens; now her son takes up the pen; the Abbé adds his paragraph; even the simple girl--la petite personne--is not afraid to pipe up on the same page. The month of May, 1678, at Les Rochers in Brittany, thus echoes with different voices. There are the birds singing; Pilois is planting; Madame de Sévigné roams the woods alone; her daughter is entertaining politicians in Provence; not very far away Monsieur de Rochefoucauld is engaged in telling the truth with Madame de La Fayette to prune his words; Racine is finishing the play which soon they will all be hearing together; and discussing afterwards with the King and that lady whom in the private language of their set they call Quanto. The voices mingle; they are all talking together in the garden in 1678. But what was happening outside?

THE HUMANE ART (* Written in April 1940.)

If at this moment there is little chance of re-reading the sixteen volumes of the Paget Toynbee edition of Walpole's letters, while the prospect of possessing the magnificent Yale edition, where all the letters are to be printed with all the answers, becomes remote, this sound and sober biography of Horace Walpole by Mr. Ketton-Cremer may serve at least to inspire some random thoughts about Walpole and the humane art which owes its origin to the love of friends.

But, according to his latest biographer, Horace Walpole's letters were inspired not by the love of friends but by the love of posterity. He had meant to write the history of his own times. After twenty years he gave it up, and decided to write another kind of history--a history ostensibly inspired by friends but in fact written for posterity. Thus Mann stood for politics; Gray for literature; Montagu and Lady Ossory for society. They were pegs, not friends, each chosen because he was "particularly connected . . . with one of the subjects about which he wished to enlighten and inform posterity." But if we believe that Horace Walpole was a historian in disguise, we are denying his peculiar genius as a letter writer. The letter writer is no surreptitious historian. He is a man of short range sensibility; he speaks not to the public at large but to the individual in private. All good letter writers feel the drag of the face on the other side of the age and obey it--they take as much as they give. And Horace Walpole was no exception. There is the correspondence with Cole to prove it. We can see, in Mr. Lewis's edition, how the Tory parson develops the radical and the free-thinker in Walpole, how the middle-class professional man brings to the surface the aristocrat and the amateur. If Cole had been nothing but a peg there would have been none of this echo, none of this mingling of voices. It is true that Walpole had an attitude and a style, and that his letters have a fine hard glaze upon them that preserves them, like the teeth of which he was so proud, from the little dents and rubs of familiarity. And of course--did he not insist that his letters must be kept?-- he sometimes looked over his page at the distant horizon, as Madame de Sévigné, whom he worshipped, did too, and imagined other people in times to come reading him. But that he allowed the featureless face of posterity to stand between him and the very voice and dress of his friends, how they looked and how they thought, the letters themselves with their perpetual variety deny. Open them at random. He is writing about politics--about Wilkes and Chatham and the signs of coming revolution in France; but also about a snuffbox; and a red riband; and about two very small black dogs. Voices upon the stairs interrupt him; more sightseers have come to see Caligula with his silver eyes; a spark from the fire has burnt the page he was writing; he cannot keep the pompous, style any longer, nor mend a careless phrase, and so, flexible as an eel, he winds from high politics to living faces and the past and its memories----"I tell you we should get together, and comfort ourselves with the brave days that we have known. . . . I wished for you; the same scenes strike us both, and the same kind of visions has amused us both ever since we were born." It is not thus that a man writes when his correspondent is a peg and he is thinking of posterity.

Nor again was he thinking of the great public, which, in a very few years, would have paid him handsomely for the brilliant pages that he lavished upon his friends. Was it, then, the growth of writing as a paid profession, and the change which that change of focus brought with it that led, in the nineteenth century, to the decline of this humane art? Friendship flourished, nor was there any lack of gift. Who could have described a party more brilliantly than Macaulay or a landscape more exquisitely than Tennyson? But there, looking them full in the face was the present moment--the great gluttonous public; and how can a writer turn at will from that impersonal stare to the little circle in the fire-lit room? Macaulay, writing to his sister, can no more drop his public manner than an actress can scrub her cheeks clean of paint and take her place naturally at the tea table. And Tennyson with his fear of publicity--"While I live the owls, when I die the ghouls"--left nothing more succulent for the ghoul to feed upon than a handful of dry little notes that anybody could read, or print or put under glass in a museum. News and gossip, the sticks and straws out of which the old letter writer made his nest, have been snatched away. The wireless and the telephone have intervened. The letter writer has nothing now to build with except what is most private; and how monotonous after a page or two the intensity of the very private becomes! We long that Keats even should cease to talk about Fanny, and that Elizabeth and Robert Browning should slam the door of the sick room and take a breath of fresh air in an omnibus. Instead of letters posterity will have confessions, diaries, notebooks, like M. Gide's-- hybrid books in which the writer talks in the dark to himself about himself for a generation yet to be born.

Horace Walpole suffered none of these drawbacks. If he was the greatest of English letter writers it was not only thanks to his gifts but to his immense good fortune. He had his places to begin with--an income of £2,500 dropped yearly into his mouth from Collectorships and Usherships and was swallowed without a pang. ". . . nor can I think myself," he wrote serenely, "as a placeman a more useless or a less legal engrosser of part of the wealth of the nation than deans and prebendaries"--indeed the money was well invested. But besides those places, there was the other--his place in the very centre of the audience, facing the stage. There he could sit and see without being seen; contemplate without being called upon to act. Above all he was blessed in his little public--a circle that surrounded him with that warm climate in which he could live the life of incessant changes which is the breath of a letter writer's existence. Besides the wit and the anecdote and the brilliant descriptions of masquerades and midnight revelries his friends drew from him something superficial yet profound, something changing yet entire-- himself shall we call it in default of one word for that which friends elicit but the great public kills? From that sprang his immortality. For a self that goes on changing is a self that goes on living. As an historian he would have stagnated among historians. But as a letter writer he buffets his way among the crowd, holding out a hand to each generation in turn--laughed at, criticized, despised, admired, but always in touch with the living. When Macaulay met him in October 1833, he struck that hand away in a burst of righteous indignation. "His mind was a bundle of inconstant whims and affectations. His features were covered by mask within mask." His letters, like PATÉ DE FOIE GRAS, owed their excellence "to the diseases of the wretched animal which furnishes it"--such was Macaulay's greeting. And what greater boon can any writer ask than to be trounced by Lord Macaulay? We take the reputation he has gored, repair it and give it another spin and another direction--another lease of life. Opinion, as Mr. Ketton-Cremer says, is always changing about Walpole. "The present age looks upon him with a more friendly eye" than the last. Is it that the present age is deafened with boom and blatancy? Does it hear in Walpole's low tones things that are more interesting, more penetrating, more true than can be said by the loud speakers? Certainly there is something wonderful to the present age in the sight of a whole human being--of a man so blessed that he could unfold every gift, every foible, whose long life spreads like a great lake reflecting houses and friends and wars and snuff boxes and revolutions and lap dogs, the great and the little, all intermingled, and behind them a stretch of the serene blue sky. "Nor will [death] I think see me very unwilling to go with him, though I have no disappointments, but I came into the world so early, and have seen so much that I am satisfied." Satisfied with his life in the flesh, he could be still more satisfied with his life in the spirit. Even now he is being collected and pieced together, letter and answer, himself and the reflections of himself, so that whoever else may die, Horace Walpole is immortal. Whatever ruin may befall the map of Europe in years to come, there will still be people, it is consoling to reflect, to hang absorbed over the map of one human face.

TWO ANTIQUARIES: WALPOLE AND COLE

Since to criticize the Yale edition of Horace Walpole's letters to Cole is impossible, for there cannot in the whole universe exist a single human being whose praise or blame of such minute and monumental learning can be of any value--if such exists his knowledge has been tapped already--the only course for the reader is to say nothing about the learning and the industry, the devotion and the skill which have created these two huge volumes, and to record merely such fleeting thoughts as have formed in the mind from a single reading. To encourage our selves, let us assert, though not with entire confidence, that books after all exist to be read--even the most learned of editors would to some extent at least agree with that. But how, the question immediately arises, can we read this magnificent instalment--for these are but the first two volumes of this edition in which Mr. Lewis will give us the complete correspondence--of our old friend Horace Walpole's letters? Ought not the presses to have issued in a supplementary pocket a supplementary pair of eyes? Then, with the usual pair fixed upon the text, the additional pair could range the notes, thus sweeping together into one haul not only what Horace is saying to Cole and what Cole is saying to Horace, but a multitude of minor men and matters: for example, Thomas Farmer, who ran away and left two girls with child; Thomas Wood, who was never drunk but had a bad constitution and was therefore left fifty pounds and bed and furniture in Cole's will; Cole's broken leg, how it was broken, and why it was badly mended; Birch, who had (it is thought) an apoplectic fit riding in the Hampstead Road, fell from his horse, and died; Thomas Western (1695-1754), who was one of the pall-bearers at the funeral of Cole's father; Cole's niece, the daughter of a wholesale cheesemonger; John Woodyer, a man of placid disposition and great probity; Mrs. Allen Hopkins, who was born Mary Thornhill; and, Lord Montfort, who--but if we want to know more about that nobleman, his lions and tigers and his "high-spirited and riotous behaviour," we must look it up for ourselves in the Harwicke MSS. in the British Museum. There are limits even to Mr. Lewis.

This little haul, taken at random, is enough to show how great a strain the new method of editing lays upon the eye. But if the brain is at first inclined to jib at such perpetual solicitations, and to beg to be allowed to read the text in peace, it adjusts itself by degrees; grudgingly admits that many of these little facts are to the point; and finally becomes not merely a convert but a suppliant--asks not for less but for more and more and more. Why, to take one instance only, is not the name of Cole's temporary cook's sister divulged? Thomas Wood was his servant; Thomas was left fifty pounds and allowed Cole's coach to run away; Thomas's younger brother James, known as "Jem," ran errands successfully and had a child ready to be sworn to him; their sister, Molly, was for one month at least a cook and helped in the kitchen. But there was another sister and, after learning all about the Woods, it is positively painful not to know at least her

Christian name.

Yet it may be asked, what has the name of Cole's cook's sister got to do with Horace Walpole? That is a question which it is impossible to answer briefly; but it is proof of the editor's triumph, justification of his system, and a complete vindication of his immense labour that he has convinced us, long before the end, that somehow or other it all hangs together. The only way to read letters is to read them thus stereoscopically. Horace is partly Cole; Cole is partly Horace; Cole's cook is partly Cole; therefore Horace Walpole is partly Cole's cook's sister. Horace, the whole Horace, is made up of innumerable facts and reflections of facts. Each is infinitely minute; yet each is essential to the other. To elicit them and relate them is out of the question. Let us, then, concentrate for a moment upon the two main figures, in outline.

We have here, then, in conjunction the Honourable Horace Walpole and the Reverend William Cole. But they were two very different people. Cole, it is true, had been at Eton with Horace, where he was called by the famous Walpole group "Tozhy," but he was not a member of that group, and socially he was greatly Walpole's inferior. His father was a farmer, Horace's father was a Prime Minister. Cole's niece was the daughter of a cheesemonger; Horace's niece married a Prince of the Blood Royal. But Cole was a man of solid good sense who made no bones of this disparity, and, after leaving Eton and Cambridge, he had become, in his quiet frequently flooded parsonage, one of the first antiquaries of the time. It was this common passion that brought the two friends together again.

For some reason, obscurely hidden in the psychology of the human race, the middle years of that eighteenth century which seems now a haven of bright calm and serene civilization, affected some who actually lived in it with a longing to escape--from its politics, from its wars, from its follies, from its drabness and its dullness, to the superior charms of the Middle Ages. "I ... hope," wrote Cole in 1765, "by the latter end of the week to be among my admired friends of the twelfth or thirteenth century. Indeed you judge very right concerning my indifference about what is going forward in the world, where I live in it as though I was no way concerned about it except in paying, with my contemporaries, the usual taxes and impositions. In good truth I am very indifferent about my Lord Bute or Mr. Pitt, as I have long been convinced and satisfied in my own mind that all oppositions are from the ins and the outs, and that power and wealth and dignity are the things struggled for, not the good of the whole. . . . I hope what I have said will not be offensive." Only one weekly newspaper, the CAMBRIDGE CHRONICLE, brought him news of the present moment. There at Bletchley or at Milton he sat secluded, wrapped up from the least draught, for he was terribly subject to sore throats; sometimes issuing forth to conduct a service, for he was, incidentally, a clergyman; driving occasionally to Cambridge to hobnob with his cronies; but always returning with delight to his study, where he copied maps, filled in coats of arms, and pored assiduously over those budgets of old manuscripts which were, as he said, "wife and children" to him. Now and again, it is true, he looked out of the window at the antics of his dog, for whose future he was careful to provide, or at those guinea fowl whose eggs he begged off Horace--for "I have so few amusements and can see these creatures from my study window when I can't stir out of my room."

But neither dog nor guinea fowl seriously distracted him. The hundred and fourteen folio volumes left by him to the British Museum testify to his professional industry. And it was precisely that quality--his professional industry--that brought the two so dissimilar men together. For Horace Walpole was by temperament an amateur. He was not, Cole admitted, "a true, genuine antiquary"; nor did he think himself one. "Then I have a wicked quality in an antiquary, nay one that annihilates the essence; that is, I cannot bring myself to a habit of minute accuracy about very indifferent points," Horace admitted. ". . . I bequeath free leave of correction to the microscopic intellects of my continuators." But he had what Cole lacked--imagination, taste, style, in addition to a passion for the romantic past, so long as that romantic past was also a civilized past, for mere "bumps in the ground" or "barrows and tumuli and Roman camps" bored him to death. Above all, he had a purse long enough to give visible and tangible expression--in prints, in gates, in Gothic temples, in bowers, in old manuscripts, in a thousand gimcracks and "brittle transitory relics" to the smouldering and inarticulate passion that drove the professional antiquary to delve like some indefatigable mole underground in the darkness of the past. Horace liked his brittle relics to be pretty, and to be authentic, and he was always eager to be put on the track of more.

The greater part of the correspondence thus is concerned with antiquaries' gossip; with parish registers and cartularies; with coats of arms and the Christian names of bishops; with the marriages of kings' daughters; skeletons and prints; old gold rings found in a field; dates and genealogies; antique chairs in Fen farmhouses; bits of stained glass and old Apostle spoons. For Horace was furnishing Strawberry Hill; and Cole was prodigiously adept at stuffing it, until there was scarcely room to stick another knife or fork, and the gorged owner of all this priceless lumber had to cry out: "I shudder when the bell rings at the gate. It is as bad as keeping an inn." All the week he was plagued with staring crowds.

Were this all it would be, and indeed it sometimes is, a little monotonous. But they were two very different men. They struck unexpected sparks in one another. Cole's Walpole was not Conway's Walpole; nor was Walpole's Cole the good-natured old parson of the diary. Cole, of course, stressed the antiquary in Walpole; but he also brought out very clearly the limits of the antiquary in Walpole. Against Cole's monolithic passion his own appears frivolous and flimsy. On the other hand, in contrast with Cole's slow-plodding pen, his own shows its mettle. He cannot flash, it is true--the subject, say, the names of Edward the Fourth's daughters, forbids it--yet how sweetly English sings on his side of the page, now in a colloquialism--"a more flannel climate"--that Cole would never have ventured; now in a strain of natural music--"Methinks as we grow old, our only business here is to adorn the graves of our friends or to dig our own." That strain was called forth by the death of their common friend, Thomas Gray. It was a death that struck at Cole's heart, too, but produced no such echo in that robust organ. At the mere threat of Conway's death, Horace was all of a twitter--his nerves were "so aspen." It was a threat only; "Still has it operated such a revolution in my mind, as no time, AT MY AGE, can efface. I have had dreams in which I thought I wished for fame--. . . I feel, I feel it was confined to the memory of those I love"--to which Cole replies: "For both your sakes I hope he will soon get well again. It is a misfortune to have so much sensibility in one's nature as you are endued with: sufficient are one's own distresses without the additional encumbrance of those of one's friends."

Nevertheless, Cole was by no means without distresses of his own. There was that terrible occasion when the horses ran away and his hat blew off and he sat with his legs in the air anticipating either death at the tollgate or a bad cold. Mercifully both were spared him. Again, he suffered tortures when, showing Dr. Gulston his prints, he begged him, as a matter of form, to take any he liked; whereupon Gulston--"that Algerine hog"--filled his portfolio with the most priceless. It is true that Cole made him pay for them in the end, but it was a most distressing business. And then what an agony it was when some fellow antiquaries dined with him, and, confined with the gout, he had to let them visit his study alone, to find next morning that an octavo volume, and a borrowed volume at that, was missing! "The Master is too honourable to take such a step," but--he had his suspicions. And what was he to do? To confess the loss or to conceal it? To conceal it seemed better, and yet, if the owner found out, "I am undone." Horace was all sympathy. He loathed the whole tribe of antiquaries--"numskulls" he called them mumbling manuscripts with their toothless jaws. "Their understandings seem as much in ruins as the things they describe," he wrote. "I love antiquities, but I scarce ever knew an antiquary who knew how to write upon them."

He had all the aristocrat's contempt for the professional drudge, and no desire whatsoever to be included among the sacred band of professional authors. "They are always in earnest, and think their profession serious, and dwell upon trifles, and reverence learning," he snapped out. And yet, when writing to Cole he could confess what to a man of his own class he would have concealed--that he, too, reverenced learning when it was real, and admired no one more than a poet if he were genuine. "A page in a great author humbles me to the dust," he wrote. And after deriding his contemporaries added, "Don't think me scornful. Recollect that I have seen Pope, and lived with Gray."

Certainly Cole's obscure but bulky form revealed a side of Horace Walpole that was lost in the glitter of the great world. With that solid man of no social gift but prodigious erudition Horace showed himself not an antiquary, not a poet, not an historian, but what he was--the aristocrat of letters, the born expert who knew the sham intellect from the genuine as surely as the antiquary knew the faked genealogy from the authentic. When Horace Walpole praised Pope and Gray he knew what he was saying and meant it; and his shame at being hoisted into such high society as theirs rings true. "I know not how others feel on such occasions, but if anyone happens to praise me, all my faults gush into my face, and make me turn my eyes inward and outward with horror. What am I but a poor old skeleton, tottering towards the grave, and conscious of ten thousand weaknesses, follies, and worse! And for talents, what are mine, but trifling and superficial; and, compared with those of men of real genius, most diminutive! . . . Does it become us, at past threescore each, to be saying fine things to one another? Consider how soon we shall both be nothing!" That is a tone of voice that he does not use in speaking--for his writing voice was a speaking voice--to his friends in the great world.

Again, Cole's High Church and Tory convictions when they touched a very different vein in Walpole sometimes caused explosions. Once or twice the friends almost came to blows over religion. The Church of England had a substantial place in Cole's esteem. But to Walpole, "Church and presbytery are human nonsense invented by knaves to govern fools. EXALTED NOTIONS OF CHURCH MATTERS are contradictions in terms to the lowliness and humility of the gospel. There is nothing sublime but the Divinity. Nothing is sacred but as His work. A tree or a brute stone is more respectable as such, than a mortal called an archbishop, or an edifice called a church, which are the puny and perishable productions of men. . . . A Gothic church or convent fill one with romantic dreams--but for the mysterious, the Church in the abstract, it is a jargon that means nothing or a great deal too much, and I reject it and its apostles from Athanasius to Bishop Keene." Those were outspoken words to a friend who wore a black coat. Yet they were not suffered to break up an intimacy of forty years. Cole, to whom Walpole's little weaknesses were not unknown, contented himself by commenting sardonically at the end of the letter upon the lowliness and humility of the aristocracy, observed that "Mr. Walpole is piqued, I can see, at my reflections on Abbot's flattery"; but in his reply to Mr. Walpole he referred only to the weather, Mr. Tyson, and the gout.

Horace's politics were equally detestable to Cole. He was, in writing at least, a red-hot republican, the bitter enemy of all those Tory principles that Cole revered. That, again, was a difference that sometimes raised the temperature of the letters to fever heat--happily for us, for it allows us, reading over their shoulders, to see Horace Walpole roused--the dilettante become a man of action, chafing at his own inactivity "sitting with one's arms folded" in a chair; deploring his country's danger; remembering that if Cole is a country clergyman, he is a Walpole; the son of a Prime Minister; that his father's son might have done more than fill Strawberry Hill with Gothic ornaments; and that his father's reputation is extremely dear to him. And yet did not gossip whisper that he was not his father's son, and was there not, somewhere deep within him, an uneasy suspicion that there was a blot on his scutcheon, a freakish strain in his clear Norfolk blood?

Whoever his father may have been, his mother nature had somehow queered the pitch of that very complex human being who was called Horace Walpole. He was not simple; he was not single. As Cole noted with antiquarian particularity, Mr. Walpole's letter of Friday, May 21St, 1762, was sealed with a "seal of red wax, a cupid with a large mask of a monkey's face. An antique. Oval." The cupid and the monkey had each set their stamp on Horace Walpole's wax. He was mischievous and obscene; he gibbered and mocked and pelted the holy shrines with nutshells. And yet with what a grace he did it--with what ease and brilliancy and wit! In body, too, he was a contradiction--lean as a grasshopper, yet tough as steel. He was lapped in luxury, yet never wore a great-coat, ate and drank as little as a fasting friar, and walked on wet grass in slippers. He fribbled away his time collecting bric-a-brac and drinking tea with old ladies; yet wrote the best letters in the language in the midst of the chatter; knew everyone; went everywhere; and, as he said, "lived post." He seemed sometimes as heartless as a monkey; drove Chatterton, so people said, to suicide, and allowed old Madame du Deffand to die alone in despair. And yet who but Cupid wrote when Gray was dead, "I treated him insolently; he loved me and I did not think he did"? Or again, "One loves to find people care for one, when they can have no view in it"? But it is futile to make such contradictions clash. There were a thousand subtler impressions stamped on the wax of Horace Walpole, and it is only posterity, for whom he had a great affection, who will be able, when they have read all that he wrote to Mann and Conway and Gray and the sisters Berry and Madame du Deffand and a score of others; and what they wrote to him; and the innumerable notes at the bottom of the page about cooks and scullions and gardeners and old women in inns--it is only they who will be able, when Mr. Lewis has brought his magnificent work to an end, to say what indeed Horace Walpole was. Meanwhile, we, who only catch a fleeting glimpse and set down hastily what we make of it, can testify that he is the best company in the world--the most amusing, the most intriguing--the strangest mixture of ape and Cupid that ever was.

THE REV WILLIAM COLE (* Written in 1932.)

A LETTER

My Dear William,

In my opinion you are keeping something back. Last year when you went to Paris and did not see Madame du Deffand but measured the exact length of every nose on every tombstone--I can assure you they have grown no longer or shorter since--I was annoyed, I admit. But I had the sense to see that, after all, you were alive, and a clergyman, and from Bletchley--in fact, you were as much out of place in Paris as a cowslip impaled upon the diamond horns of a duchess's tiara. Put him back in Bletchley, I said, plant him in his own soil, let him burble on in his own fashion, and the miracle will happen. The cows will low; the church bells will ring; all Bletchley will come alive; and, reading over William's shoulder, we shall see deep, deep into the hearts of Mrs. Willis and Mr. Robinson.

I regret to tell you that I was wrong. You are not a cowslip. You do not bloom. The hearts of Mrs. Willis and Mr. Robinson remain sealed books to us. You write January 16th, 1766, and it is precisely as if I had written January 16th, 1932. In other words, you have rubbed all the bloom off two hundred years and that is so rare a feat--it implies something so queer in the writer--that I am intrigued and puzzled and cannot help asking you to enlighten me. Are you simply a bore, William? No that is out of the question. In the first place, Horace Walpole did not tolerate bores, or write to them, or go for country jaunts with them; in the second, Miss Waddell loves you. You shed all round you, in the eyes of Miss Waddell, that mysterious charm which those we love impart to their meanest belongings. She loves your parrot; she commiserates your cat. Every room in your house is familiar to her. She knows about your Gothic chamber and your neat arched bed; she knows how many steps led up to the pantry and down to the summer house; she knows, she approves, how you spent every hour of your day. She sees the neighbours through the light of your eyes. She laughs at some; she likes others; she knows who was fat and who was thin, and who told lies, who had a bad leg, and who was no better than she should have been. Mr. and Mrs. Barton, Thomas Tansley, Mr. and Mrs. Lord of Mursley, the Diceys, and Dr. Pettingal are all real and alive to her: so are your roses, your horses, your nectarines and your knats.

Would that I could see through her eyes! Alas, wherever I look I see blight and mildew. The moss never grows upon your walls. Your nectarines never ripen. The blackbird sings, but out of tune. The knats--and you say "I hardly know a place so pestered with that vermin as Bletchley"--bite, just like our gnats. As for the human beings they pass through the same disenchantment. Not that I have any fault to find with your friends or with Bletchley either. Nobody is very good, but then nobody is very bad. Tom sometimes hits a hare, oftener he misses; the fish sometimes bite, but not always; if it freezes it also thaws, and though the harvest was not bad it might have been better. But now, William, confess. We know in our hearts, you and I, that England in the eighteenth century was not like this. We know from Woodforde, from Walpole, from Thomas Turner, from Skinner, from Gray, from Fielding, from Jane Austen, from scores of memoirs and letters, from a thousand forgotten stone masons, bricklayers and cabinet makers, from a myriad sources, that I have not learning to name or space to quote, that England was a substantial, beautiful country in the eighteenth century; aristocratic and common; hand-made and horse-ploughed; an eating, drinking, bastard-begetting, laughing, cursing, humorous, eccentric, lovable land. If with your pen in your hand and the dates facing you, January 16th, 1766, you see none of all this, then the fault is yours. Some spite has drawn a veil across your eyes. Indeed, there are pouches under them I could swear. You slouch as you walk. You switch at thistles half-heartedly with your stick. You do not much enjoy your food. Gossip has no relish for you. You mention the "scandalous story of Mr. Felton Hervey, his two daughters and a favourite footman" and add, "I hope it is not true." So do I, but I cannot put much life into my hoping when you withhold the facts. You stop Pettingal in the middle of his boasting--you cut him short with a sarcasm--just as he was proving that the Greeks liked toasted cheese and was deriving the word Bergamy from the Arabic. As for Madame Geoffrin, you never lose a chance of saying something disobliging about that lady; a coffee-pot has only to be reputed French for you to defame it. Then look how touchy you are--you grumble, the servants are late with the papers, you complain, Mr. Pitt never thanked you for the pigeons (yet Horace Walpole thought you a philosopher); then how you suspect people's motives; how you bid fathers thrash their little boys; how you are sure the servant steals the onions. All these are marks of a thin-blooded poverty-stricken disposition. And yet--you are a good man; you visit the poor; you bury the infected; you have been educated at Cambridge; you venerate antiquity. The truth is that you are concealing something, even from Miss Waddell.

Why, I ask, did you write this diary and lock it in a chest with iron hoops and insist that no one was to read it or publish it for twenty years after your death unless it were that you had something on your mind, something that you wished to confess and get rid of? You are not one of those people who love life so well that they cherish even the memory of roast mutton, like Woodforde; you did not hate life so much that you must shriek out your curse on it, Eke poor Skinner. You write and write, ramblingly, listlessly, like a person who is trying to bring himself to say the thing that will explain to himself what is wrong with himself. And you find it very hard. You would rather mention anything but that--Miss Chester, I mean, and the boat on the Avon. You cannot force yourself to admit that you have kept that lock of hair in your drawer these thirty years. When Mrs. Robinson, her daughter, asked you for it (March 19th 1766) you said you could not find it. But you were not easy under that concealment. You did at length go to your private drawer (November 26th, 1766) and there it was, as you well knew.

But even so, with the lock of hair in your hand, you still seek to put us off the scent. You ramble on about giving Mrs. Robinson a barrel of oysters; about potted rabbits; about the weather, until suddenly out it comes, "Gave Mrs. Robinson a braided Lock of Lady Robinson's Mother's hair (and Sister to Mrs. Robinson of Cransley), which I cut off in a Boat on the River Avon at Bath about 30 years ago when my Sister Jane and myself were much acquainted with her, then Miss Chester." There we have it. The poisoned tooth is out. You were once young and ardent and very much in love. Passion overcame you. You were alone. The wind blew a lock of Miss Chester's hair from beneath her hat. You reached forward. You cut it. And then? Nothing. That is your tragedy--you yourself failed yourself. You think of that scene twenty times a day, I believe, as you saunter, rather heavily; along the damp paths at Bletchley. That is the dreary little tune that you hum as you stoop over your parments measuring noses, deciphering dates--"I failed, failed, failed on the boat on the Avon." That is why your nectarines are blighted; and the parrot dies; and the parlour cat is scalded; and you love nobody except, perhaps, your little dun-coloured horse. That is why you "always had a mind to live retired in Glamorganshire." That is why Mr. Pitt never thanked you for the pigeons. That is why Mr. Stonehewer became His Majesty's Historiographer, while you visited paupers in Fenny Stratford. That is why he never came to see you, and why you observed so bitterly, that "people suffer themselves to forget their old friends when they are surrounded by the great and are got above the world." You see, William, if you hoard a failure, if you come to grudge even the sun for shining--and that, I think, is what you did--fruit does not ripen; a blight falls upon parrots and cats; people would actually rather that you did not give them pigeons.

But enough. I may be wrong. Miss Chester's hair may have nothing to do with it. And Miss Waddell may be right--every good quality of heart and head may be yours. I am sure I hope so. But I beg, William, now that you are about to begin a fresh volume, at Cambridge too, with men of character and learning, that you will pull yourself together. Speak out. Justify the faith that Miss Waddell has in you. For you are keeping one of the finest scholars of her time shut up in the British Museum among mummies and policemen and wet umbrellas. There must be a trifle of ninety-five volumes more of you in those iron-bound chests. Lighten her task; relieve our anxiety, and so add to the gratitude of your obliged obedient servant,

Virginia Woolf.

THE HISTORIAN AND "THE GIBBON" (* Written in March 1937.)

"Yet, upon the whole, the HISTORY OF THE DECLINE AND FALL seems to have struck root, both at home and abroad, and may, perhaps, a hundred years hence still continue to be abused." So Gibbon wrote in the calm confidence of immortality; and let us confirm him in his own opinion of his book by showing, in the first place, that it has one quality of permanence--it still excites abuse. Few people can read the whole of the DECLINE AND FALL without admitting that some chapters have glided away without leaving a trace; that many pages are no more than a concussion of sonorous sounds; and that innumerable figures have passed across the stage without printing even their names upon our memories. We seem, for hours on end, mounted on a celestial rocking-horse which, as it gently sways up and down, remains rooted to a single spot. In the soporific idleness thus induced we recall with regret the vivid partisanship of Macaulay, the fitful and violent poetry of Carlyle. We suspect that the vast fame with which the great historian is surrounded is one of those vague diffusions of acquiescence which gather when people are too busy, too lazy or too timid to see things for themselves. And to justify this suspicion it is easy to gather pomposities of diction--the Church has become "the sacred edifice"; and sentences so stereotyped that they chime like bells--"destroyed the confidence" must be followed by "and excited the resentment"; while characters are daubed in with single epithets like "the vicious" or "the virtuous," and are so crudely jointed that they seem capable only of the extreme antics of puppets dangling from a string. It is easy, in short, to suppose that Gibbon owed some part of his fame to the gratitude of journalists on whom he bestowed the gift of a style singularly open to imitation and well adapted to invest little ideas with large bodies. And then we turn to the book again, and to our amazement we find that the rocking-horse has left the ground; we are mounted on a winged steed; we are sweeping in wide circles through the air and below us Europe unfolds; the ages change and pass; a miracle has taken place.

But miracle is not a word to use in writing of Gibbon. If miracle there was it lay in the inexplicable fact which Gibbon, who seldom stresses a word, himself thought worthy of italics: ". . . I KNOW by experience, that from my early youth I aspired to the character of an historian." Once that seed was planted so mysteriously in the sickly boy whose erudition amazed his tutor there was more of the rational than of the miraculous in the process by which that gift was developed and brought to fruition. Nothing, in the first place, could have been more cautious, more deliberate and more far-sighted than Gibbon's choice of a subject. A historian he had to be; but historian of what? The history of the Swiss was rejected; the history of Florence was rejected; for a long time he played with the idea of a life of Sir Walter Raleigh. Then that, too, was rejected and for reasons that are extremely illuminating:

...I should shrink with terror from the modern history of England, where every character is a problem, and every reader a friend or an enemy; where a writer is supposed to hoist a flag of party, and is devoted to damnation by the adverse faction.... I must embrace a safer and more extensive theme.

But once found, how was he to treat the distant, the safe, the extensive theme? An attitude, a style had to be adopted; one presumably that generalized, since problems of character were to be avoided; that abolished the writer's personality, since he was not dealing with his own times and contemporary questions; that was rhythmical and fluent, rather than abrupt and intense, since vast stretches of time had to be covered, and the reader carried smoothly through many folios of print.

At last the problem was solved; the fusion was complete; matter and manner became one; we forget the style, and are only aware that we are safe in the keeping of a great artist. He is able to make us see what he wants us to see and in the right proportions. Here he compresses; there he expands. He transposes, emphasizes, omits in the interests of order and drama. The features of the individual faces are singularly conventionalized. Here are none of those violent gestures and unmistakable voices that fill the pages of Carlyle and Macaulay with living human beings who are related to ourselves. There are no Whigs and Tories here; no eternal verities and implacable destinies. Time has cut off those quick reactions that make us love and hate. The innumerable figures are suffused in the equal blue of the far distance. They rise and fall and pass away without exciting our pity or our anger. But if the figures are small, they are innumerable; if the scene is dim it is vast. Armies wheel; hordes of barbarians are destroyed; forests are huge and dark; processions are splendid; altars rise and fall; one dynasty succeeds another. The richness, the variety of the scene absorb us. He is the most resourceful of entertainers. Without haste or effort he swings his lantern where he chooses. If sometimes the size of the whole is oppressive, and the unemphatic story monotonous, suddenly in the flash of a phrase a detail is lit up: we see the monks "in the lazy gloom of their convents"; statues become unforgettably "that inanimate people"; the "gilt and variegated armour" shines out: the splendid names of kings and countries are sonorously intoned; or the narrative parts and a scene opens:

By the order of Probus, a great quantity of large trees, torn up by the roots, were transplanted into the midst of the circus. The spacious and shady forest was immediately filled with a thousand ostriches, a thousand stags, a thousand fallow deer, and a thousand wild boars; and all this variety of game was abandoned to the riotous impetuosity of the multitude.... The air was continually refreshed by the playing of fountains, and profusely impregnated by the grateful scent of aromatics. In the centre of the edifice, the arena, or stage, was strewed with the finest sand, and successively assumed the most different forms. At one moment it seemed to rise out of the earth, like the garden of Hesperides, and was afterwards broken into the rocks and caverns of Thrace. . . .

But it is only when we come to compress and dismember one of Gibbon's pictures that we realize how carefully the parts have been chosen, how firmly the sentences, composed after a certain number of turns round the room and then tested by the ear and only then written down, adhere together.

But these are qualities, it might be said, that belong to the historical novelist--to Scott or to Flaubert. And Gibbon was an historian, so religiously devoted to the truth that he felt an aspersion upon his accuracy as an aspersion upon his character. Flights of notes at the bottom of the page check his pageants and verify his characters. Thus they have a different quality from scenes and characters composed from a thousand hints and suggestions in the freedom of the imagination. They are inferior, perhaps, in subtlety and in intensity. On the other hand, as Gibbon pointed out, "The Cyropaedia is vague and languid; the Anabasis circumstantial and animated. Such is the eternal difference between fiction and truth."

The imagination of the novelist must often fail; but the historian can repose himself upon fact. And even if those facts are sometimes dubious and capable of more than one interpretation, they bring the reason into play and widen our range of interest. The vanished generations, invisible separately, have collectively spun round them intricate laws, erected marvellous structures of ceremony and belief. These can be described, analysed, recorded. The interest with which we follow him in his patient and impartial examination has an excitement peculiar to itself. History may be, as he tells us, "little more than the register of the crimes, follies, and misfortunes of mankind"; but we seem, at least, as we read him raised above the tumult and the chaos into a clear and rational air.

The victories and the civilization of Constantine no longer influence the state of Europe; but a considerable portion of the globe still retains the impression which it received from the conversion of that monarch; and the ecclesiastical institutions of his reign are still connected, by an indissoluble chain, with the opinions, the passions, and the interests of the present generation.

He is not merely a master of the pageant and the story; he is also the critic and the historian of the mind.

It is here of course that we become conscious of the idiosyncrasy and of the limitations of the writer. Just as we know that Macaulay was a nineteenth-century Whig, and Carlyle a Scottish peasant with the gift of prophecy, so we know that Gibbon was rooted in the eighteenth century and indelibly stamped with its character and his own. Gradually, stealthily, with a phrase here, a gibe there, the whole solid mass is leavened with the peculiar quality of his temperament. Shades of meaning reveal themselves; the pompous language becomes delicate and exact. Sometimes a phrase is turned edgewise, so that as it slips with the usual suavity into its place it leaves a scratch. "He was even destitute of a sense of honour, which so frequently supplies the sense of public virtue." Or the solemn rise and fall of the text above is neatly diminished by the demure particularity of a note. "The ostrich's neck is three feet long, and composed of seventeen vertebrae. See Buffon. Hist. Naturelle." The infallibility of historians is gravely mocked. "... their knowledge will appear gradually to increase, as their means of information must have diminished, a circumstance which frequently occurs in historical disquisitions." Or we are urbanely asked to reflect how,

in our present state of existence, the body is so inseparably connected with the soul, that it seems to be to our interest to taste, with innocence and moderation, the enjoyments of which that faithful companion is susceptible.

The infirmities of that faithful companion provide him with a fund of perpetual amusement. Sex, for some reason connected, perhaps, with his private life, always excites a demure smile:

Twenty-two acknowledged concubines, and a library of sixty-two thousand volumes, attested the variety of his inclinations; and from the productions which he left behind him, it appears that the former as well as the latter were designed for use rather than for ostentation.

The change upon such phrases is rung again and again. Few virgins or matrons, nuns or monks leave his pages with their honour entirely unscathed. But his most insidious raillery, his most relentless reason, are directed, of course, against the Christian religion.

Fanaticism, asceticism, superstition were naturally antipathetic to him. Wherever he found them, in life or in religion, they roused his contempt and derision. The two famous chapters in which he examined "the HUMAN causes of the progress and establishment of Christianity," though inspired by the same love of truth which in other connections excited the admiration of scholars, roused great scandal at the time. Even the eighteenth century, that "age of light and liberty," was not entirely open to the voice of reason. "How many souls have his writings polluted!" Hannah More exclaimed when she heard of his death. "Lord preserve others from their contagion!" In such circumstances irony was the obvious weapon; the pressure of public opinion forced him to be covert, not open. And irony is a dangerous weapon; it easily becomes sidelong and furtive; the ironist seems to be darting a poisoned tongue from a place of concealment. However grave and temperate Gibbon's irony at its best, however searching his logic and robust his contempt for the cruelty and intolerance of superstition, we sometimes feel, as he pursues his victim with incessant scorn, that he is a little limited, a little superficial, a little earthy, a little too positively and imperturbably a man of the eighteenth century and not of our own.

But then he is Gibbon; and even historians, as Professor Bury reminds us, have to be themselves. History "is in the last resort somebody's image of the past, and the image is conditioned by the mind and experience of the person who forms it." Without his satire, his irreverence, his mixture of sedateness and slyness, of majesty and mobility, and above all that belief in reason which pervades the whole book and gives it unity, an implicit if unspoken message, the

DECLINE AND FALL would be the work of another man. It would be the work indeed of two other men. For as we read we are perpetually creating another book, perceiving another figure. The sublime person of "the historian" as the Sheffields called him is attended by a companion whom they called, as if he were the solitary specimen of some extinct race, "the Gibbon." The Historian and the Gibbon go hand in hand. But it is not easy to draw even a thumbnail sketch of this strange being because the autobiography, or rather the six autobiographies, compose a portrait of such masterly completeness and authority that it defies our attempts to add to it. And yet no autobiography is ever final; there is always something for the reader to add from another angle.

There is the body, in the first place--the body with all those little physical peculiarities that the outsider sees and uses to interpret what lies within. The body in Gibbon's case was ridiculous--prodigiously fat, enormously top-heavy, precariously balanced upon little feet upon which he spun round with astonishing alacrity. Like Goldsmith he over-dressed, and for the same reason perhaps--to supply the dignity which nature denied him. But unlike Goldsmith, his ugliness caused him no embarrassment or, if so, he had mastered it completely. He talked incessantly, and in sentences composed as carefully as his writing. To the sharp and irreverent eyes of contemporaries his vanity was perceptible and ridiculous; but it was only on the surface. There was something hard and muscular in the obese little body which turned aside the sneers of the fine gentlemen.

He had roughed it, not only in the Hampshire Militia, but among his equals. He had supped "at little tables covered with a napkin, in the middle of a coffee room, upon a bit of cold meat or a Sandwich," with twenty or thirty of the first men in the kingdom, before he retired to rule supreme over the first families of Lausanne. It was in London, among the distractions of society and politics, that he achieved that perfect poise, that perfect balance between work, society and the pleasures of the senses which composed his wholly satisfactory existence. And the balance had not been arrived at without a struggle. He was sickly; he had a spendthrift for a father; he was expelled from Oxford; his love affair was thwarted; he was short of money and had none of the advantages of birth. But he turned everything to profit. From his lack of health he learnt the love of books; from the barrack and the guardroom he learnt to understand the common people; from his exile he learnt the smallness of the English cloister; and from poverty and obscurity how to cultivate the amenities of human intercourse.

At last it seemed as if life itself were powerless to unseat this perfect master of her uncertain paces. The final buffet-
-the loss of his sinecure--was turned to supreme advantage; a perfect house, a perfect friend, a perfect society at once placed themselves at his service, and without loss of time or temper Gibbon entered a post-chaise with Caplin his valet and Muff his dog and bowled over Westminster Bridge to finish his history and enjoy his maturity in circumstances that were ideal.

But as we run over the familiar picture there is something that eludes us. It may be that we have not been able to find out anything for ourselves. Gibbon has always been before us. His self-knowledge was consummate; he had no illusions either about himself or about his work. He had chosen his part and he played it to perfection. Even that characteristic attitude, with his snuff-box in his hand and his body stretched out, he had noted himself, and perhaps he had adopted it as consciously as he observed it. But it is his silence that is most baffling. Even in the letters, where he drops the Historian and shortens himself now and then to "the Gib," there are long pauses when nothing is heard even at Sheffield Place of what is going on in the study at Lausanne.

The artist after all is a solitary being. Twenty years spent in the society of the DECLINE AND FALL are twenty years spent in solitary communion with distant events, with intricate problems of arrangement, with the minds and bodies of the dead. Much that is important to other people loses its importance; the perspective is changed when the eyes are fixed not upon the foreground but upon the mountains, not upon a living woman but upon "my other wife, the DECLINE AND FALL OF THE ROMAN EMPIRE." And it is difficult, after casting firm sentences that will withstand the tread of time. to say "in three words, I am alone." It is only now and then that we catch a phrase that has not been stylized, or see a little picture that he has not been able to include in the majestic design. For example, when Lord Sheffield bursts out in his downright way, "You are a right good friend . . .," we see the obese little man impetuously and impulsively hoisting himself into a post-chaise and crossing a Europe ravaged by revolution to comfort a widower. And again when the old stepmother at Bath takes up her pen and quavers out a few uncomposed and unliterary sentences we see him:

I truely rejoice, & congratulate you on your being once more safely arrived in your native Country. I wish'd to tell you so yesterday, but the joy your letter gave would not suffer my hand to be steady enough to write. . . . Many has been the disappointments I have borne with fortitude, but the fear of having my last and only friend torn from me was very near overseting my reason. . . . Madame Ely and Mrs. Bonfoy are here. Mrs. Holroyd has probably told you that Miss Gould is now Mrs. Horneck. I wish she had been Mrs. Gibbon . . .

so the old lady rambles on, and for a moment we see him as in a cracked mirror held in a trembling hand. For a moment, a cloud crosses that august countenance. It was true. He had sometimes on returning home in the evening, sighed for a companion. He had sometimes felt that "domestic solitude . . . is a comfortless state." He had conceived the romantic idea of adopting and educating a young female relative called Charlotte. But there were difficulties; the idea was abandoned. Then the cloud drifts away; common sense, indomitable cheerfulness return; once more the serene figure of the historian emerges triumphant. He had every reason to be content. The great building was complete; the mountain was off his breast; the slave was freed from the toil of the oar.

And he was by no means exhausted. Other tasks less laborious, perhaps more delightful, lay before him. His love of literature was unsated; his love of life--of the young, of the innocent, of the gay--was unblunted. It was the faithful companion, the body, unfortunately, that failed him. But his composure was unshaken. He faced death with an equanimity that speaks well for "the profane virtues of sincerity and moderation." And as he sank into a sleep that was probably eternal, he could remember with satisfaction the view across the plain to the stupendous mountains beyond; the white acacia that grew beside the study window, and the great work which, he was not wrong in thinking, will immortalize his name.

REFLECTIONS AT SHEFFIELD PLACE
(* Written in May 1937.)

The great ponds at Sheffield Place at the right season of the year are bordered with red, white and purple reflections, for rhododendrons are massed upon the banks and when the wind passes over the real flowers the water flowers shake and break into each other. But there, in an opening among the trees stands a great fantastic house, and since it was there that John Holroyd, Lord Sheffield, lived, since it was there that Gibbon stayed, another reflection imposes itself upon the water trance. Did the historian himself ever pause here to cast a phrase, and if so what words would he have found for those same floating flowers? Great lord of language as he was, no doubt he filled his mind from the fountain of natural beauty. The exactions of the DECLINE AND FALL meant, of course, the death and dismissal of many words deserving of immortal life. Order and seemliness were drastically imposed. It was a question, he reflected, "whether some flowers of fancy, some grateful errors, have not been eradicated with the weeds of prejudice." Still his mind was a whispering gallery of words; the famous "barefooted friars" singing vespers may have been a recollection of Marlowe's "And ducke as low as any bare-foot Fryar," murmuring in the background. Be this as it may, to consider what Gibbon would have said had he seen the rhododendrons reflected in the water is an idle exercise, for in his day, late in the eighteenth century, a girl who looked out of the window of Sheffield Place saw not rhododendrons "but four young swans . . . now entirely grey" floating upon the water. Moreover, it is unlikely that he ever bestirred himself to walk in the grounds. "Gib," that same girl, Maria Josepha Holroyd, remarked, "is a mortal enemy to any person taking a walk, and he is so frigid that he makes us sit by a good roasting Christmas fire every evening." There he sat in the summer evening talking endlessly, delightfully, in the best of spirits, for no place was more like home to him than Sheffield Place, and he looked upon the Holroyds as his own flesh and blood.

Seen through Maria's eyes Gibbon--she called him sometimes "Gib," sometimes "le grand Gibbon," sometimes "The Historian"--looked different from Gibbon seen by himself. In 1792 she was a girl of twenty-one; he was a man of fifty-five. To him she was "the tall and blooming Maria"; "the soft and stately Maria," a niece by adoption, whose manners he could correct; whose future he could forecast--"That establishment must be splendid; that life must be happy"; whose style, especially one metaphor about the Rhine escaping its banks, he could approve. But to her he was often an object of ridicule; he was so fat; such a figure of fun "waddling across the room whenever she [Madame da Silva] appeared, and sitting by her and looking at her, till his round eyes run down with water"; rather testy too, an old bachelor, who lived like clockwork and hated to have his plans upset; but at the same time, she had to admit, the most delightful of talkers. That summer night he drew out the two young men who were staying in the house, Fred North and Mr. Douglas, and made them far more entertaining than they would have been without him. "It was impossible to have selected three Beaux who could have been more agreeable, whether their conversation was trifling or serious," whether they talked about Greek and Latin or turtle soup. For that summer Mr. Gibbon was "raving" about turtles and wanted Lord Sheffield to have one brought from London. Maria's gaze rested upon him with a mixture of amusement and respect; but it did not rest upon him alone. For not only were Fred North and Mr. Douglas in the room, and the swans on the pond outside and the woods; but soldiers were tramping past the Park gates; the Prince himself was holding a review; they were going over to inspect the camp; Mr. Gibbon and Aunt Serena in the post chaise; she, if only her father would let her, on horseback. But the sight of her father suggested other cares; he was wildly hospitable; he had asked the Prince and the Duke to stay; and as her mother was dead, all the catering, all the entertaining fell upon her. There was too something in her father's face that made her look at Mr. Gibbon as if for support; he was the only man who could influence her father; who could bring him to reason; who could check his extravagance, restrain . . . But here she paused, for there was some weakness in her father's character that could not be put into plain language by a daughter. At any rate she was very glad when he married a second time "for I feel delighted to think when sooner or later troubles come, as we who know the gentleman must fear . . ." Whatever frailty of her father's she hinted at, Mr. Gibbon was the only one of his friends whose good sense could restrain him.

The relation between the Peer and the Historian was very singular. They were devoted. But what tie was it that attached the downright, self-confident, perhaps loose-living man of the world to the suave, erudite sedentary historian?--the attraction of opposites perhaps. Sheffield, with his finger in every pie, his outright, downright man of-the-world's good sense, supplied the historian with what he must sometimes have needed--someone to call him "you damned beast," someone to give him a solid footing on English earth. In Parliament Gibbon was dumb; in love he was ineffective. But his friend Holroyd was a member of a dozen committees; before one wife was two years in the grave he had married another. If it is true that friends are chosen partly in order to live lives that we cannot live in our own persons, then we can understand why the Peer and the Historian were devoted; why the great writer divested himself of his purple language and wrote racy colloquial English to Sheffield; why Sheffield curbed his extravagance and restrained his passions in deference to Gibbon; why Gibbon crossed Europe, in a post chaise to console Sheffield for his wife's death; and why Sheffield, though always busied with a thousand affairs of his own, yet found time to manage Gibbon's tangled money matters; and was now indeed engaged in arranging the business of Aunt Hester's legacy.

Considering Hester Gibbon's low opinion of her nephew and her own convictions it was surprising that she had left him any thing at all. To her Gibbon stood for all those lusts of the flesh, all those vanities of the intellect which many years previously she had renounced. Many years ago, many years before the summer night when they sat round the fire in the Library and discussed Latin and Greek and turtle soup, Hester Gibbon had put all such vanities behind her. She had left Putney and the paternal house to follow her brother's tutor William Law to his home in Northamptonshire. There in the village of King's Cliffe she lived with him trying to understand his mystic philosophy, more successfully putting it into practice; teaching the ignorant; living frugally; feeding beggars, spending her substance on charity. There at last, for she made no haste to join the Saints as her nephew observed, at the age of eighty-six she lay by Law's side in his grave; while Mrs. Hutcheson, who had shared his house but not his love, lay in an inferior position at their feet. Every difference that could divide two human beings seems to have divided the aunt from the nephew; and yet they had something in common. The suburban world of Putney had called her mad because she believed too much; the learned world of divinity had called him wicked because he believed too little. Both aunt and nephew found it impossible to hit off the exact degree of scepticism and belief which the world holds reasonable. And this very difference perhaps had not been without its effect upon the nephew. When he was a young man practising the graces which were to conciliate the world he adored, his eccentric aunt had roused his ridicule. "Her dress and figure exceed anything we had at the masquerade; her language and ideas belong to the last century," he wrote. In fact, though his urbanity never deserted him in writing to her--he was her heir-at-law we are reminded--his comments to others upon the Saint, the Holy Matron of Northamptonshire, as he called her, were of an acutely ironical kind; nor did he fail to note maliciously those little frailties--her anger when Mrs. Hutcheson forgot her in her will; her reprehensible desire to borrow from a nephew whom she refused to meet--which were to him so marked a feature of the saintly temper, so frequent an accompaniment of a mind clouded by enthusiasm. As Maria Holroyd observed, and others have observed after her, the great historian had a round mouth but an extremely pointed tongue; and--who knows?--it may have been Aunt Hester herself who first sharpened that weapon. Edward's father, for instance, may have talked about William Law, his tutor--an admirable man of course; far too great a man, to have been the tutor of a scatter-brained spendthrift like himself; still William Law had made himself very comfortable at the Gibbon's house in Putney, had filled it with his own friends; had allowed Hester to fall passionately in love with him, but had never married her, since marriage was against his creed--had only accepted her devotion and her income, conduct which in another might have been condemned--so he may have gossiped. From very early days at any rate Edward must have had a private view of the eccentricities of the unworldly, of the inconsistencies of the devout. At last, however, Aunt Hester, as her nephew irreverently remarked, had "gone to sing Hallelujahs." She lay with William Law in the grave, after a life of what ecstasies, of what tortures, of what jealousies, of what safisfactions who can say? The only fact that was certain was that she had left one hundred pounds and an estate at Newhaven to her "poor though unbelieving nephew." "She might have done better, she might have done worse," he observed. And by an odd coincidence her land lay not far from the Holroyd property; Lord Sheffield was eager to buy it. He could easily pay for it, he was sure, by cutting down some of the timber.

If then we accept Aunt Hester's view, Gibbon was a worldling, wallowing in the vanities of the flesh, scoffing at the holiness of the faith. But his other aunt, his mother's sister, took a very different view of him. To his Aunt Kitty he had been ever since he was a babe a source of acute anxiety--he was so weakly; and of intense pride--he was such a prodigy. His mother was one of those flyaway women who make great use of their unmarried sisters, since they are frequently in childbed themselves and have an appetite for pleasure when they can escape the cares of the nursery. She died, moreover, in her prime; and Kitty of course took charge of the only survivor of all those cradles, nursed him, petted him, and was the first to inspire him with that love of pagan literature which was to bring the glitter of minarets and the flash of eastern pageantry so splendidly into his sometimes too pale and pompous prose. It was Aunt Kitty who, with a prodigality that would have scandalized Aunt Hester, flung open the door of that enchanted world-- the world of THE CAVERN OF THE WINDS, of the PALACE OF FELICITY, of Pope's HOMER, and of the

ARABIAN NIGHTS in which Edward was to roam for ever. "Where a title attracted my eye, without fear or awe I snatched the volume from the shelf; and Mrs. Porten, who indulged herself in moral and religious speculations, was more prone to encourage. than to check a curiosity above the strength of a boy." And it was she who first loosened his lips. "Her indulgent tenderness, the frankness of her temper, and my innate rising curiosity, soon removed all distance between us; like friends of an equal age, we freely conversed on every topic, familiar or abstruse." It was she who began the conversation which was still continuing in front of the fire in the library that summer night.

What would have happened if the child had fallen into the hands of his other aunt and her companion? Should we have had the DECLINE AND FALL if they had controlled his reading and checked his curiosity, as William Law checked all reading and condemned all curiosity? It is an interesting question. But the effect on the man of his two incompatible aunts developed a conflict in his nature. Aunt Hester, from whom he expected a fortune, encouraged, it would seem from his letters, a streak of hypocrisy, a vein of smooth and calculating conventionality. He sneered to Sheffield at her religion; when she died he hailed her departure with a flippant joke. Aunt Kitty on the other hand brought out a strain of piety, of filial devotion. When she died he wrote, as if it were she and not the Saint who made him think kindly for a moment of Christianity, "The immortality of the soul is on some occasions a very comfortable doctrine." And it was she certainly who made him bethink him when she was asked to stay at Sheffield Place, that "Aunt Kitty has a secret wish to lye in my room; if it is not occupied, it might be indulged." So while Aunt Hester lay with William Law in the grave, Aunt Kitty hoisted herself into the great four-poster with the help of the stool which the little man always used, and lay there, seeing the very cupboards and chairs that her nephew saw when he slept there, and the pond perhaps and the trees out of the window. The great historian, whose gaze swept far horizons and surveyed the processions of the Roman Emperors, could also fix them minutely upon a rather tedious old lady and guess her fancy to sleep in a certain bed. He was a strange mixture.

Very strange, Maria may have thought as she sat there listening to his talk while she stitched: selfish yet tender; ridiculous but sublime. Perhaps human nature was like that--by no means all of a piece; different at different moments; changing, as the furniture changed in the firelight, as the waters of the lake changed when the night wind swept over them. But it was time for bed; the party broke up. Mr. Gibbon, she noted with concern, for she was genuinely fond of him, had some difficulty in climbing the stairs. He was unwell; a slight operation for an old complaint was necessary, and he left them with regret to go to town. The operation was over; the news was good; they hoped that he would soon be with them again. Then suddenly between five and six of a January evening an express arrived at Sheffield Place to say that he was dangerously ill. Lord Sheffield and his sister

Serena started immediately for London. It was fine, luckily, and the moon was up. "The night was light as day," Serena wrote to Maria. "The beauty of it was solemn and almost melancholy with our train of ideas, but it seemed to calm our minds." They reached Gibbon's lodging at midnight and "poor Dussot came to the door the picture of despair to tell me HE was no more. . . ." He had died that morning; he was already laid in the shell of his coffin. A few days later they brought him back to Sheffield Place; carried him through the Park, past the ponds, and laid him under a crimson cloth among the Holroyds in the Mausoleum.

As for the "soft and stately Maria" she survived to the year 1863; and her granddaughter Kate, the mother of Bertrand Russell, marvelled that an old woman of that age should mind dying--an old woman who had lived through the French Revolution, who had entertained Gibbon at Sheffield Place.

THE MAN AT THE GATE
(* Written in September 1940.)

The man was Coleridge as De Quincey saw him, standing in a gateway. For it is vain to put the single word Coleridge at the head of a page--Coleridge the innumerable, the mutable, the atmospheric; Coleridge who is part of Wordsworth, Keats and Shelley; of his age and of our own; Coleridge whose written words fill hundreds of pages and overflow innumerable margins; whose spoken words still reverberate, so that as we enter his radius he seems not a man, but a swarm, a cloud, a buzz of words, darting this way and that, clustering, quivering and hanging suspended. So little of this can be caught in any reader's net that it is well before we become dazed in the labyrinth of what we call Coleridge to have a clear picture before us--the picture of a man standing at a gate:

. . . his person was broad and full, and tended even to corpulence, his complexion was fair . . . his eyes were large and soft in their expression; and it was from the peculiar appearance of haze or dreaminess which mixed with their light, that I recognized my object.

That was in 1807. Coleridge was already incapable of movement. The Kendal black drop had robbed him of his will. "You bid me rouse myself--go, bid a man paralytic in both arms rub them briskly together." The arms already hung flabby at his side; he was powerless to raise them. But the disease which paralysed his will left his mind unfettered.

143

In proportion as he became incapable of action, he became capable of feeling. As he stood at the gate his vast expanse of being was a passive target for innumerable arrows, all of them sharp, many of them poisoned. To confess, to analyse, to describe was the only alleviation of his appalling torture-- the prisoner's only means of escape.

Thus there shapes itself in the volumes of Coleridge's letters an immense mass of quivering matter, as if the swarm had attached itself to a bough and hung there pendent. Sentences roll like drops down a pane, drop collecting drop, but when they reach the bottom, the pane is smeared. A great novelist, Dickens for preference, could have formed out of this swarm and diffusion a prodigious, an immortal character. Dickens, could he have been induced to listen, would have noted--perhaps this:

Deeply wounded by very disrespectful words used concerning me, and which struggling as I have been thro' life, and still maintaining a character and holding connections no way unworthy of my Family

Or again:

The worst part of the charges were that I had been imprudent enough and in the second place gross and indelicate enough to send out a gentleman's servant in his own house to a public house for a bottle of brandy . . .

Or again:

What joy would it not be to you or to me, Miss Betham! to meet a Milton in a future state

And again, on accepting a loan:

I can barely collect myself sufficiently to convey to you- -first, that I receive this proof of your filial kindness with feelings not unworthy of the same ... but that, whenever (if ever) my circumstances shall improve, you must permit me to remind you that what was, and FOREVER under ALL conditions of fortune will be, FELT as a GIFT, has become a Loan--and lastly, that you must let me have you as a frequent friend on whose visits I may rely as often as convenience will permit you ...

The very voice (drastically cut short) of Micawber himself!

But there is a difference. For this Micawber knows that he is Micawber. He holds a looking-glass in his hand. He is a man of exaggerated self-consciousness, endowed with an astonishing power of self-analysis. Dickens would need to be doubled with Henry James, to be trebled with Proust, in order to convey the complexity and the conflict of a Pecksniff who despises his own hypocrisy, of a Micawber who is humiliated by his own humiliation. He is so made that he can hear the crepitation of a leaf, and yet remains obtuse to the claims of wife and child. An unopened letter brings great drops of sweat to his forehead; yet to lift a pen and answer it is beyond his power. The Dickens Coleridge and the Henry James Coleridge perpetually tear him asunder. The one sends out surreptitiously to Mr. Dunn the chemist for another bottle of opium; and the other analyses the motives that have led to this hypocrisy into an infinity of fine shreds.

Thus often in reading the "gallop scrawl" of the letters

from Highgate in 1820 we seem to be reading notes for a late work by Henry James. He is the forerunner of all who have tried to reveal the intricacies, to take the faintest creases of the human soul. The great sentences pocketed with parentheses, expanded with dash after dash, break their walls under the strain of including and qualifying and suggesting all that Coleridge feels, fears and glimpses. Often he is prolix to the verge of incoherence, and his meaning dwindles and fades to a wisp on the mind's horizon. Yet in our tongue-tied age there is a joy in this reckless abandonment to the glory of words. Cajoled, caressed, tossed up in handfuls, words yield those flashing phrases that hang like ripe fruit in the many-leaved tree of his immense volubility. "Brow-hanging, shoe-contemplative, STRANGE"; there is Hazlitt. Of Dr. Darwin: "He was like a pigeon picking up peas, and afterwards voiding them with excremental additions." Anything may tumble out of that great maw; the subtlest criticism, the wildest jest, the exact condition of his intestines. But he uses words most often to express the crepitations of his apprehensive susceptibility. They serve as a smoke-screen between him and the menace of the real world. The word screen trembles and shivers. What enemy is approaching? Nothing visible to the naked eye. And yet how he trembles and quivers! Hartley, "poor Hartley . . . in shrinking from the momentary pain of telling the plain truth, a truth not discreditable to him or to me, has several times inflicted an agitating pain and confusion"--by what breach of morality or dereliction of duty?--"by bringing up Mr. Bourton unexpectedly on Sundays with the intention of dining here." Is that all? Ah, but a diseased body feels the stab of anguish if only a corn is trod upon. Anguish shoots through every fibre of his being. Has he not himself often shrunk from the momentary pain of telling the plain truth? Why has he no home to offer his son, no table to which Hartley could bring his friends uninvited? Why does he live a stranger in the house of friends, and be (at present) unable to discharge his share of the housekeeping expenses? The old train of bitter thoughts is set in motion once more. He is one hum and vibration of painful emotion. And then, giving it all the slip, he takes refuge in thought and provides Hartley with "in short, the sum of all my reading and reflections on the vast Wheel of the Mythology of the earliest and purest Heathenism." Hartley must feed upon that and take a snack of cold meat and pickles at some inn.

Letter-writing was in its way a substitute for opium. In his letters he could persuade others to believe what he did not altogether believe himself--that he had actually written the folios, the quartos, the octavos that he had planned. Letters also relieved him of those perpetually pullulating ideas which, like Surinam toads, as he said, were always giving birth to little toads that "grow quickly and draw off attention from the mother toad." In letters thoughts need not be brought to a conclusion. Somebody was always interrupting, and then he could throw down his pen and indulge in what was, after all, better than writing--the "insemination" of ideas without the intermediary of any gross impediment by word of mouth into the receptive, the acquiescent, the entirely passive ear, say, of Mr. Green who arrived punctually at three. Later, if it were Thursday, in came politicians, economists, musicians, business men, fine ladies, children--it mattered not who they were so long as he could talk and they would listen.

Two pious American editors have collected the comments of this various company, (* COLERIDGE THE TALKER. Edited by Richard W. Armour and Raymond F. Howes.) and they are, of course, various. Yet it is the only way of getting at the truth--to have it broken into many splinters by many mirrors and so select. The truth about Coleridge the talker seems to have been that he rapt some listeners to the seventh heaven; bored others to extinction; and made one foolish girl giggle irrepressibly. In the same way his eyes were brown to some, grey to others, and again a very bright blue. But there is one point upon which all who listened are agreed; not one of them could remember a single word he said. All, however, with astonishing unanimity are agreed that it was "like"-- the waves of the ocean, the flowing of a mighty river, the splendour of the Aurora Borealis, the radiance of the Milky Way. Almost all are equally agreed that waves, river, Borealis, and Milky Way lacked, as Lady Jerningham tersely put it, "behind." From their accounts it is clear that he avoided contradiction; detested personality; cared nothing who you were; only needed some sound of breathing or rustle of skirts to stir his flocks of dreaming thoughts into motion and light the glitter and magic that lay sunk in the torpid flesh. Was it the mixture of body and mind in his talk that gave off some hypnotic fume that lulled the audience into drowsiness? He acted as he talked; now, if he felt the interest flag, pointing to a picture, or caressing a child, and then, as the time to make an exit approached, majestically possessed himself of a bedroom candlestick and, still discoursing, disappeared. Thus played upon by gesture and voice, brow and glittering eye, no one, as Crabb Robinson remarks, could take a note. It is then in his letters, where the body of the actor was suppressed, that we have the best record of the siren's song. There we hear the voice that began talking at the age of two--"Nasty Doctor Young" are his first recorded words; and went on in barracks, on board ship, in pulpits, in stage coaches--it mattered not where he found himself or with whom, Keats it might be or the baker's boy--on he went, on and on, talking about nightingales, dreams, the will, the volition, the reason, the understanding, monsters, and mermaids, until a little girl, overcome by the magic of the incantation, burst into tears when the voice ceased and left her alone in a silent world.

We too, when the voice stops only half an hour before he passed that July day in 1834 into silence, feel bereft. Is it for hours or for years that this heavily built man standing in a gate has been pouring forth this passionate soliloquy, while his "large soft eyes with a peculiar expression of haze or dreaminess mixed in their light" have been fixed upon a far-away vision that filled a very few pages with poems in which every word is exact and every image as clear as crystal?

SARA COLERIDGE
(* Written in September 1940.)

Coleridge also left children of his body. One, his daughter, Sara, was a continuation of him, not of his flesh inded, for she was minute, aetherial, but of his mind, his temperament. The whole of her forty-eight years were lived in the light of his sunset, so that, like other children of great men, she is a chequered dappled figure flitting between a vanished radiance and the light of every day. And, like so many of her father's works, Sara Coleridge remains unfinished. Mr. Griggs (* COLERIDGE FILLE: A BIOGRAPHY OF SARA COLERIDGE. By Earl Leslie Griggs.) has written her life, exhaustively, sympathetically; but still . . . dots intervene. That extremely interesting fragment, her autobiography, ends with three rows of dots after twenty-six pages. She intended, she says, to end every section with a moral, or a reflection. And then "on reviewing my earlier childhood I find the predominant reflection. . . ." There she stops. But she said many things in those twenty-six pages, and Mr. Griggs has added others that tempt us to fill in the dots, though not with the facts that she might have given us.

"Send me the very feel of her sweet Flesh, the very look and motion of that mouth--O, I could drive myself mad about her," Coleridge wrote when she was a baby. She was a lovely child, delicate, large-eyed, musing but active, very still but always in motion, like one of her father's poems. She remembered how he took her as a child to stay with the

Wordsworths at Allan Bank.

The rough farmhouse life was distasteful to her, and to her shame they bathed her in a room where men came in and out. Delicately dressed in lace and muslin, for her father liked white for girls, she was a contrast to Dora, with her wild eyes and floating yellow hair and frock of deep Prussian blue or purple--for Wordsworth liked clothes to be coloured. The visit was full of such contrasts and conflicts. Her father cherished her and petted her. "I slept with him and he would tell me fairy stories when he came to bed at twelve or one o'clock...."Then her mother, Mrs. Coleridge, arrived, and Sara flew to that honest, homely, motherly woman and "wished never to be separated from her." At that--the memory was still bitter--"my father showed displeasure and accused me of want of affection. I could not understand why.... I think my father's motive," she reflected later, "must have been a wish to fasten my affections on him.... I slunk away and hid myself in the wood behind the house."

But it was her father who, when she lay awake terrified by a horse with eyes of flame, gave her a candle. He, too, had been afraid of the dark. With his candle beside her, she lost her fear, and lay awake, listening to the sound of the river, to the thud of the forge hammer, and to the cries of stray animals in the fields. The sounds haunted her all her life. No country, no garden, no house ever compared with the Fells and the horse-shoe lawn and the room with three windows looking over the lake to the mountains. She sat there while her father, Wordsworth and De Quincey paced up and down talking. What they said she could not understand, but she "used to note the handkerchief hanging out of the pocket and long to clutch it." When she was a child the handkerchief vanished and her father with it. After that, "I never lived with him for more than a few weeks at a time," she wrote. A room at Greta Hall was always kept ready for him but he never came. Then the brothers, Hartley and Derwent, vanished, too; and Mrs. Coleridge and Sara stayed on with Uncle Southey, feeling their dependence and resenting it. "A house of bondage Greta Hall was to her," Hartley wrote. Yet there was Uncle Southey's library; and thanks to that admirable, erudite and indefatigable man, Sara became mistress of six languages, translated Dobritzhoffer from the Latin, to help pay for Hartley's education, and qualified herself, should the worst come, to earn her living. "Should it be necessary," Wordsworth wrote, "she will be well fitted to become a governess in a nobleman's or gentleman's family. . . . She is remarkably clever."

But it was her beauty that took her father by surprise when at last at the age of twenty she visited him at Highgate. She was learned he knew, and he was proud of it; but he was unprepared, Mr. Griggs says, "for the dazzling vision of loveliness which stepped across the threshold one cold December day." People rose in a public hall when she came in. "I have seen Miss Coleridge," Lamb wrote, "and I wish I had just such a--daughter." Did Coleridge wish to keep such a daughter? Was a father's jealousy roused in that will-less man of inordinate susceptibility when Sara met her cousin

Henry up at Highgate and almost instantly, but secretly, gave him her coral necklace in exchange for a ring with his hair? What right had a father who could not offer his daughter even a room to be told of the engagement or to object to it? He could only quiver with innumerable conflicting sensations at the thought that his nephew, whose book on the West Indies had impressed him unfavourably, was taking from him the daughter who, like Christabel, was his masterpiece, but, like Christabel, was unfinished. All he could do was to cast his magic spell. He talked. For the first time since she was a woman, Sara heard him talk. She could not remember a word of it afterwards. And she was penitent. It was partly that

my father generally discoursed on such a very extensive scale.... Henry could sometimes bring him down to narrower topics, but when alone with me he was almost always on the star-paved road, taking in the whole heavens in his circuit.

She was a heaven-haunter, too; but at the moment "I was anxious about my brothers and their prospects--about Henry's health, and upon the subject of my engagement generally." Her father ignored such things. Sara's mind wandered.

The young couple, however, made ample amends for that momentary inattention. They listened to his voice for the rest of their lives. At the christening of their first child Coleridge talked for six hours without stopping. Hard-worked as Henry was, and delicate, sociable and pleasure-loving, the spell of Uncle Sam was on him, and so long as he lived he helped his wife. He annotated, he edited, he set down what he could remember of the wonderful voice. But the main labour fell on Sara. She made herself, she said, the housekeeper in that littered palace. She followed his reading; verified his quotations; defended his character; traced notes on innumerable margins; ransacked bundles; pieced beginnings together and supplied them not with ends but with continuations. A whole day's work would result in one erasure. Cab fares to newspaper offices mounted; eyes, for she could not afford a secretary, felt the strain; but so long as a page remained obscure, a date doubtful, a reference unverified, an aspersion not disproved, "poor, dear, indefatigable Sara," as Mrs. Wordsworth called her, worked on. And much of her work was done lastingly; editors still stand on the foundations she truly laid.

Much of it was not self-sacrifice, but self-realization. She found her father, in those blurred pages, as she had not found him in the flesh; and she found that he was herself. She did not copy him, she insisted; she was him. Often she continued his thoughts as if they had been her own. Did she not even shuffle a little in her walk, as he did, from side to side? Yet though she spent half her time in reflecting that vanished radiance, the other half was spent in the light of common day--at Chester Place, Regents Park. Children were born and children died. Her health broke down; she had her father's legacy of harassed nerves; and, like her farther, had need of opium. Pathetically she wished that she could be given "three years' respite from child bearing." But she wished in vain.

Then Henry, whose gaiety had so often dragged her from the dark abyss, died young; leaving his notes unfinished, and two children also, and very little money, and many apartments in Uncle Sam's great house still unswept.

She worked on. In her desolation it was her solace, her opium perhaps. "Things of the mind and intellect give me intense pleasure; they delight and amuse me as they are in themselves . . . and sometimes I think, the result has been too large, the harvest too abundant, in inward satisfaction. This is dangerous. . . ." Thoughts proliferated. Like her father she had a Surinam toad in her head, breeding other toads. But his were jewelled; hers were plain. She was diffuse, unable to conclude, and without the magic that does instead of a conclusion. She would have liked, had she been able to make an end, to have written--on metaphysics, on theology, some book of criticism. Or again, politics interested her intensely, and Turner's pictures. But "whatever subject I commence, I feel discomfort unless I could pursue it in every direction to the farthest bounds of thought. . . . This was the reason why my father wrote by snatches. He could not bear to complete incompletely." So, book in hand, pen suspended, large eyes filled with a dreamy haze, she mused--"picking flowers, and finding nests, and exploring some particular nook, as I used to be when a child walking with my Uncle Southey. . . ."

Then her children interrupted. With her son, the brilliant Herbert, she read, straight through the classics. Were there not, Mr. Justice Coleridge objected, passages in Aristophanes that they had better skip? Perhaps. . . . Still, Herbert took all the prizes, won all the scholarships, almost drove her to distraction with his horn-playing and, like his father, loved parties. Sara went to balls, and watched him dance waltz after waltz. She had the old lovely clothes that Henry had given her altered for her daughter, Edith. She found herself eating supper twice, she was so bored. She preferred dinner parties where she held her own with Macaulay, who was so like her father in the face, and with Carlyle--"A precious Arch-charlatan," she called him. The young poets, like Aubrey de Vere, sought her out. She was one of those, he said, "whose thoughts are growing while they speak." After he had gone, her thoughts followed him, in long, long letters, rambling over baptism, regenerations, metaphysics, theology, and poetry, past, present and to come. As a critic she never, like her father, grazed paths of light; she was a fertilizer, not a creator, a burrowing, tunnelling reader, throwing up molehills as she read her way through Dante, Virgil, Aristophanes, Crashaw, Jane Austen, Crabbe, to emerge suddenly, unafraid, in the very face of Keats and Shelley. "Fain would mine eyes," she wrote, "discern the Future in the past."

Past, present, future dappled her with a strange light. She was mixed in herself, still divided, as in the wood behind the house, between two loyalties, to the father who told her fairy stories in bed; and to the mother--Frettikins she called her--to whom she clung in the flesh. "Dear mother," she exclaimed, "what an honest, simple, lively minded affectionate woman she was, how free from disguise or artifice. . . ." Why, even her wig--she had cut her hair off as a girl--"was as dry and rough and dull as a piece of stubble, and as short and stumpy." The wig and the brow--she understood them both. Could she have skipped the moral she could have told us much about that strange marriage. She meant to write her life. But she was interrupted. There was a lump on her breast. Mr. Gilman, consulted, detected cancer. She did not want to die. She had not finished editing her father's works, she had not written her own, for she did not like to complete incompletely. But she died at forty-eight, leaving, like her father, a blank page covered with dots, and two lines:

Father, no amaranths e'er shall wreathe my brow--
Enough that round thy grave they flourish now.

"NOT ONE OF US"
(* A review of SHELLEY; HIS LIFT AND WORK. By Walter Edwin Peck, October 1927.)

Professor Peck does not apologize for writing a new life of Shelley, nor does he give any reason for doing what has been so thoroughly done already, nor are the new documents that have come into his hands of any great importance. And yet nobody is going to complain that here are two more thick, illustrated, careful and conscientious volumes devoted to the retelling of a story which everyone knows by heart. There are some stories which have to be retold by each generation, not that we have anything new to add to them, but because of some queer quality in them which makes them not only Shelley's story but our own. Eminent and durable they stand on the skyline, a mark past which we sail, which moves as we move and yet remains the same.

Many such changes of orientation toward Shelley have been recorded. In his own lifetime all except five people looked upon him, Shelley said, "as a rare prodigy of crime and pollution, whose look even might infect." Sixty years later he was canonized by Edward Dowden. By Matthew Arnold he was again reduced to the ordinary human scale. How many biographers and essayists have since absolved him or sentenced him, it is impossible to say. And now comes our turn to make up our minds what manner of man Shelley was; so that we read Professor Peck's volumes, not to find out new facts, but to get Shelley more sharply outlined against the shifting image of ourselves.

If such is our purpose, never was there a biographer who gave his readers more opportunity to fulfil it than Professor Peck. He is singularly dispassionate, and yet not colourless. He has opinions, but he does not obtrude them. His attitude to Shelley is kind but not condescending. He does not rhapsodize, but at the same time he does not scold. There are only two points which he seems to plead with any personal partiality; one, that Harriet was a much wronged woman; the other, that the political importance of Shelley's poetry is not rated sufficiently high. Perhaps we could spare the careful analysis of so many poems. We scarcely need to know how many times mountains and precipices are mentioned in the course of Shelley's works. But as a chronicler of great learning and lucidity, Professor Peck is admirable. Here, he seems to say, is all that is actually known about Shelley's life. In October he did this in November he did that; now it was that he wrote this poem it was here that he met that friend. And, moulding the enormous mass of the Shelley papers with dexterous fingers, he contrives tactfully to embed dates and facts in feelings, in comments, in what Shelley wrote, in what Mary wrote, in what other people wrote about them, so that we seem to be breasting the full current of Shelley's life and get the illusion that we are, this time, seeing Shelley, not through the rosy glasses or the livid glasses which sentiment and prudery have fixed on our forerunners' noses, but plainly, as he was. In this, of course, we are mistaken; glasses we wear, though we cannot see them. But the illusion of seeing

Shelley plain is sufficiently exhilarating to tempt us to try to fix it while it lasts.

There is an image of Shelley's personal appearance in everybody's picture gallery. He was a lean, large-boned boy, much freckled, with big, rather prominent blue eyes. His dress was careless, of course, but it was distinguished; "he wore his clothes like a gentleman." He was courteous and gentle in manner, but he spoke in a shrill, harsh voice and soon rose to the heights of excitement. Nobody could overlook the presence of this discordant character in the room, and his presence was strangely disturbing. It was not merely that he might do something extreme, he might, somehow, make whoever was there appear absurd. From the earliest days normal people had noticed his abnormality and had done their best, following some obscure instinct of self-preservation, to make Shelley either toe the line or else quit the society of the respectable. At Eton they called him "mad Shelley" and pelted him with muddy balls. At Oxford he spilt acid over his tutor's carpet, "a new purchase, which he thus completely destroyed," and for other and more serious differences of opinion he was expelled.

After that he became the champion of every down-trodden cause and person. Now it was an embankment; now a publisher; now the Irish nation; now three poor weavers condemned for treason; now a flock of neglected sheep. Spinsters of all sorts who were oppressed or aspiring found in him their leader. The first years of his youth thus were spent in dropping seditious pamphlets into old women's hoods; in shooting scabby sheep to put them out of their misery; in raising money; in writing pamphlets; in rowing out to sea and dropping bottles into the water which when broken open by the Town Clerk of Barnstable were found to contain a seditious paper, "the contents of which the mayor has not yet been able to ascertain." In all these wanderings and peregrinations he was accompanied by a woman, or perhaps by two women, who either had young children at the breast or were shortly expecting to become mothers. And one of them, it is said, could not contain her amusement when she saw the pamphlet dropped into the old woman's hood, but burst out laughing.

The picture is familiar enough; the only thing that changes is our attitude toward it. Shelley, excitable, uncompromising, atheistical, throwing his pamphlets into the sea in the belief that he is going to reform the world, has become a figure which is half heroic and wholly delightful. On the other hand, the world that Shelley fought has become ridiculous. Somehow the untidy, shrill-voiced boy, with his violence and his oddity has succeeded in making Eton and Oxford, the English government, the Town Clerk and Mayor of Barnstable, the country gentlemen of Sussex and innumerable obscure people whom we might call generically, after Mary's censorious friends, the Booths and the Baxters--Shelley has succeeded in making all these look absurd.

But, unfortunately, though one may make bodies and institutions look absurd, it is extremely difficult to make private men and women look anything so simple. Human relationships are too complex; human nature is too subtle. Thus contact with Shelley turned Harriet Westbrook, who should have been the happy mother of a commonplace family, into a muddled and bewildered woman, who wanted both to reform the world and yet to possess a coach and bonnets, and was finally drawn from the Serpentine on a winter's morning, drowned in her despair. And Mary and Miss Hitchener, and Godwin and Claire, and Hogg and Emilia Viviani, and Sophia Stacey and Jane Williams--there is nothing tragic about them, perhaps; there is, indeed, much that is ridiculous. Still, their association with Shelley does not lead to any clear and triumphant conclusion. Was he right? Were they right? The whole relationship is muddy and obscure; it baffles; it teases.

One is reminded of the private life of another man whose power of conviction was even greater than Shelley's, and more destructive of normal human happiness. One remembers Tolstoy and his wife. The alliance of the intense belief of genius with the easy-going non-belief or compromise of ordinary humanity must, it seems, lead to disaster and to disaster of a lingering and petty kind in which the worst side of both natures is revealed. But while Tolstoy might have wrought out his philosophy alone or in a monastery, Shelley was driven by something yielding and enthusiastic in his temperament to entangle himself with men and women. "I think one is always in love with something or other," he wrote. But this "something or other" besides lodging in poetry and metaphysics and the good of society in general, had its dwelling in the bodies of human beings of the opposite sex.

He saw "the likeness of what is perhaps eternal" in the eyes of Mary. Then it vanished, to appear in the eyes of Emilia; then there it was again manifesting itself indisputably in Sophia Stacey or in Jane Williams. What is the lover to do when the will o' the wisp shifts its quarters? One must go on, said Shelley, until one is stopped. And what is to stop one? Not, if one is Shelley, the conventions and superstitions which bind the baser part of mankind; not the Booths and the Baxters. Oxford might expel him, England might exile him, but still, in spite of disaster and derision, he sought the "likeness of what is perhaps eternal"; he went on being in love.

But as the object of his love was a hybrid creature, half human, half divine, so the manner of his love partook of the same ambiguous nature. There was something inhuman about Shelley. Godwin, in answer to Shelley's first letter, noticed it. He complained of the "generalizing character" of Shelley's style, which, he said, had the effect of making him "not an individual character" to him. Mary Shelley, musing over her life when Shelley was dead, exclaimed, "What a strange life mine has been. Love, youth, fear and fearlessness led me early from the regular routine of life and I united myself to this being who, not one of US, though like us, was pursued by numberless miseries and annoyances, in all of which I shared." Shelley was "not one of us." He was, even to his wife, a "being," some one who came and went like a ghost, seeking the eternal. Of the transitory, he had little notion. The joys and sorrows, from whose threads are woven the warm cocoon of private life in which most men live, had no hold upon him. A strange formality stiffens his letters; there is no intimacy in them and no fun.

At the same time it is perfectly true, and Professor Peck does well to emphasize the fact, that Shelley loved humanity if he did not love this Harriet or that Mary. A sense of the wretchedness of human beings burnt in him as brightly and as persistently as his sense of the divine beauty of nature. He loved the clouds and the mountains and the rivers more passionately than any other man loved them; but at the foot of the mountain he always saw a ruined cottage; there were criminals in chains, hoeing up the weeds in the pavement of St. Peter's Square; there was an old woman shaking with ague on the banks of the lovely Thames. Then he would thrust aside his writing, dismiss his dreams and trudge off to physic the poor with medicine or with soup. Inevitably there collected round him, as time went on, the oddest assortment of pensioners and protégés. He took on himself the charge of deserted women and other people's children; he paid other persons' debts and planned their journeys and settled their relationships. The most ethereal of poets was the most practical of men.

Hence, says Professor Peck, from this union of poetry and humanity springs the true value of Shelley's poetry. It was the poetry of a man who was not a "pure poet," but a poet with a passion for reforming the wrongs of men. Had he lived, he would have reconciled poetry and the statement of "the necessity of certain immediate reforms in politics, society and government." He died too young to be able to deliver his message; and the difficulty of his poetry arises from the fact that the conflict between poetry and politics rages there unresolved. We may not agree with Professor Peck's definition, yet we have only to read Shelley again to come up against the difficulty of which he speaks. It lies partly in the disconcerting fact that we had thought his poetry so good and we find it indeed so poor. How are we to account for the fact that we remember him as a great poet and find him on opening his pages a bad one? The explanation seems to be that he was not a "pure poet." He did not concentrate his meaning in a small space; there is nothing in Shelley's poetry as rich and compact as the odes of Keats. His taste could be sentimental; he had all the vices of the album makers; he was unreal, strained, verbose. The lines which Professor Peck quotes with admiration: "Good night? No, love! The night is ill," seems to us a proof of it. But if we pass from the lyrics, with all their exquisite beauty, and read ourselves into one of the longer poems, EPIPSYCHIDION or PROMETHEUS UNBOUND, where the faults have space to lose themselves, we again become convinced of his greatness. And here again we are confronted by a difficulty. For if we were asked to extract the teaching from these poems we should be at a loss. We can hardly say what reform in "politics, society and government" they advocate. Their greatness seems to lie in nothing so definite as a philosophy, in nothing so pure as perfection of expression. It lies rather in a state of being. We come through skeins of clouds and gusts of whirlwind out into a space of pure calm, of intense and windless serenity. Defensibly or not, we make a distinction- -THE SKYLARK, the ODE TO THE WEST WIND are poems; the PROMETHEUS, the EPIPSYCHIDION are poetry.

So if we outline our relationship to Shelley from the vantage ground Of 1927 we shall find that his England is a barbarous place where they imprison journalists for being disrespectful to the Prince Regent, stand men in stocks for publishing attacks upon the Scriptures, execute weavers upon the suspicion of treason, and, without giving proof of strict religious belief themselves, expel a boy from Oxford for avowing his atheism. Politically, then, Shelley's England has already receded, and his fight, valiant though it is, seems to be with monsters who are a little out of date, and therefore slightly ridiculous. But privately he is much closer to us. For alongside the public battle wages, from generation to generation, another fight which is as important as the other, though much less is said about it. Husband fights with wife and son with father. The poor fight the rich and the employer fights the employed. There is a perpetual effort on the one hand to make all these relationships more reasonable, less painful and less servile; on the other, to keep them as they are. Shelley, both as son and as husband, fought for reason and freedom in private life, and his experiments, disastrous as they were in many ways, have helped us to greater sincerity and happiness in our own conflicts. The Sir Timothys of

Sussex are no longer so prompt to cut their sons off with a shilling; the Booths and the Baxters are no longer quite so sure that an unmarried wife is an unmitigated demon. The grasp of convention upon private life is no longer quite so coarse or quite so callous because of Shelley's successes and failures.

So we see Shelley through our particular pair of spectacles--a shrill, charming, angular boy; a champion riding out against the forces of superstition and brutality with heroic courage; at the same time blind, inconsiderate, obtuse to other persons' feelings. Rapt in his extraordinary vision, ascending to the very heights of existence, he seems, as Mary said, "a being," "not one of us," but better and higher and aloof and apart. Suddenly there comes a knock at the door; the Hunts and seven children are at Leghorn; Lord Byron has been rude to them; Hunt is cut to the heart. Shelley must be off at once to see that they are comfortable. And, rousing himself from his rapture, Shelley goes.

HENRY JAMES

1. WITHIN THE RIM (* Written in 1919.)

It would be easy to justify the suspicion which the sight of WITHIN THE RIM aroused, and to make it account for the tepid and formal respect with which we own to have approached the book. Essays about the war contributed to albums and books with a charitable object even by the most distinguished of writers bear for the most part such traces of perfunctory composition, such evidence of genius forcibly harnessed to the wagon of philanthropy and sullen and stubborn beneath the lash, that one is inclined for the sake of the writer to leave them unread. But we should not have said this unless we intended immediately and completely to unsay it. The process of reading these essays was a process of recantation. It is possible that the composition of some of them was an act of duty, in the sense that the writing of a chapter of a novel was not an act of duty. But the duty was imposed upon Henry James not by the persuasions of a committee nor by the solicitations of friends, but by a power much more commanding and irresistible--a power so large and of such immense significance to him that he scarcely succeeds with all his range of expression in saying what it was or all that it meant to him. It was Belgium, it was France, it was above all England and the English tradition, it was everything that he had ever cared for of civilization, beauty and art threatened with destruction and arrayed before his imagination in one figure of tragic appeal.

Perhaps no other elderly man existed in August 1914 so well qualified to feel imaginatively all that the outbreak of war meant as Henry James. For years he had been appreciating ever more and more finely what he calls "the rare, the sole, the exquisite England": he had relished her discriminatingly as only the alien, bred to different sounds and sights and circumstances, could relish others so distinct and so delightful in their distinctness. Knowing so well what she had given him, he was the more tenderly and scrupulously grateful to her for the very reason that she seemed to him to bestow her gifts half in ignorance of their value. Thus when the news came that England was in danger he wandered in the August sunshine half overwhelmed with the vastness of what had happened, reckoning up his debt, conscious to the verge of agony of the extent to which he had committed his own happiness to her, and analysing incessantly and acutely just what it all meant to the world and to him. At first, as he owned, he had "an elderly dread of a waste of emotion ... my house of the spirit amid everything around me had become more and more the inhabited, adjusted, familiar home"; but before long he found himself

building additions and upper storeys, throwing out extensions and protrusions, indulging even, all recklessly, in gables and pinnacles and battlements--things that had presently transformed the unpretending place into I scarce know what to call it, a fortress of the faith, a palace of the soul, an extravagant, bristling, flag-flying structure which had quite as much to do with the air as with the earth.

In a succession of images not to be torn from their context he paints the state of his mind confronted by one aspect after another of what appeared to him in so many diverse lights of glory and of tragedy. His gesture as of one shrinking from the sight of the distress, combined with an irresistible instinct of pity drawing him again and again to its presence, recalls to the present writer his reluctance to take a certain road in Rye because it led past the workhouse gates and forced to his notice the dismal line of tramps waiting for admittance. But in the case of the wounded and the fugitive his humanity forced him again and again to face the sight, and brought him the triumphant reward of finding that the beauty emerging from such conditions more than matched the squalor. ". . . their presence," he wrote of the wounded soldier, "is a blest renewal of faith."

A moralist perhaps might object that terms of beauty and ugliness are not the terms in which to speak of so vast a catastrophe, nor should a writer exhibit so keen a curiosity as to the tremors and vibrations of his own spirit in face of the universal calamity. Yet, of all books describing the sights of war and appealing for our pity, this largely personal account is the one that best shows the dimensions of the whole. It is not merely or even to any great extent that we have been stimulated intellectually by the genius of Henry James to analyse shades and subtleties; but rather that for the first and only time, so far as we are aware, someone has reached an eminence sufficiently high above the scene to give it its grouping and standing in the universal. Read, for instance, the scene of the arrival of the Belgian refugees by night at Rye, which we will not curtail and thus rob of its completeness. It is precisely the same little scene of refugees hurrying by in silence, save for the cry of a woman carrying her child, which, in its thousand varieties, a thousand pens have depicted during the past four years. They have done their best, and left us acknowledging their effort, but feeling it to be a kind of siege or battering ram laid to the emotions, which have obstinately refused to yield their fruits. That it is altogether otherwise with the scene painted for us by Henry James might perhaps be credited to his training as a novelist. But when, in his stately way, diminishing his stature not one whit and majestically rolling the tide of his prose over the most rocky of obstacles, he asks us for the gift of a motor-car, we cannot help feeling that if all philanthropies had such advocates our pockets would never be anything but empty. It is not that our emotions have been harassed by the sufferings of the individual case. That he can do upon occasion with beautiful effect. But what he does in this little book of less than a hundred and twenty pages is, so it seems to us, to present the best statement yet made of the largest point of view. He makes us understand what civilization meant to him and should mean to us. For him it was a spirit that overflowed the material bounds of countries, but it is in France that he sees it most plainly personified:

. . . what happens to France happens to all that part of ourselves which we are most proud, and most finely advised, to enlarge and cultivate and consecrate. . . . She is sole and single in this, that she takes charge of those of the 'interests of man which most dispose him to fraternize with himself, to pervade all his possibilities and to taste all his faculties, and in consequence to find and to make the earth a friendlier, an easier, and especially a more various sojourn.

If all our counsellors, we cannot help exclaiming, had spoken with that voice!

HENRY JAMES

2. THE OLD ORDER (* Written in 1917.)

With this small volume, (* THE MIDDLE YEARS. By Henry James.) which brings us down to about the year 1870, the memories of Henry James break off. It is more fitting to say that they break off than that they come to an end, for although we are aware that we shall hear his voice no more, there is no hint of exhaustion or of leave-taking; the tone is as rich and deliberate as if time were unending and matter infinite; what we have seems to be but the prelude to what we are to have, but a crumb, as he says, of a banquet now forever withheld. Someone speaking once incautiously in his presence of his "completed" works drew from him the emphatic assertion that never, never so long as he lived could there be any talk of completion; his work would end only with his life; and it seems in accord with this spirit that we should feel ourselves pausing, at the end of a paragraph, while in imagination the next great wave of the wonderful voice curves into fullness.

All great writers have, of course, an atmosphere in which they seem most at their ease and at their best; a mood of the great general mind which they interpret and indeed almost discover, so that we come to read them rather for that than for any story or character or scene of separate excellence. For ourselves Henry James seems most entirely in his element, doing that is to say what everything favours his doing, when it is a question of recollection. The mellow light which swims over the past, the beauty which suffuses even the commonest little figures of that time, the shadow in which the detail of so many things can be discerned which the glare of day flattens out, the depth, the richness, the calm, the humour of the whole pageant--all this seems to have been his natural atmosphere and his most abiding mood. It is the atmosphere of all those stories in which aged Europe is the background for young America. It is the half light in which he sees most, and sees farthest. To Americans, indeed, to Henry James and to Hawthorne, we owe the best relish of the past in our literature--not the past of romance and chivalry, but the immediate past of vanished dignity and faded fashions. The novels teem with it; but wonderful as they are, we are tempted to say that the memories are yet more wonderful, in that they are more exactly Henry James, and give more precisely his tone and his gesture. In them his benignity is warmer, his humour richer, his solicitude more exquisite, his recognition of beauty, fineness, humanity more instant and direct. He comes to his task with an indescribable air of one so charged and laden with precious stuff that he hardly knows how to divest himself of it all--where to find space to set down this and that, how to resist altogether the claims of some other gleaming object in the background; appearing so busy, so unwieldy with ponderous treasure that his dexterity in disposing of it, his consummate knowledge of how best to place each fragment, afford us the greatest delight that literature has had to offer for many a year. The mere sight is enough to make anyone who has ever held a pen in his hand consider his art afresh in the light of this extraordinary example of it. And our pleasure at the mere sight soon merges in the thrill with which we recognize, if not directly then by hearsay, the old world of London-life which he brings out of the shades and sets tenderly and solidly before us as if his last gift were the most perfect and precious of the treasures hoarded in "the scented chest of our savings."

After the absence from Europe of about nine years which is recorded in NOTES OF A SON AND BROTHER, he arrived in Liverpool on March 1st, 1869, and found himself "in the face of an opportunity that affected me then and there as the happiest, the most interesting, the most alluring and beguiling that could ever have opened before a somewhat disabled young man who was about to complete his twenty-sixth year." He proceeded to London, and took up his lodging with a "kind slim celibate," a Mr. Lazarus Fox- -every detail is dear to him--who let out slices of his house in Half Moon Street to gentlemen lodgers. The London of that day, as Henry James at once proceeded to ascertain with those amazingly delicate and tenacious tentacles of his, was an extremely characteristic and uncompromising organism. "The big broom of change" had swept it hardly at all since the days of Byron at least. She was still the "unaccommodating and unaccommodated city . . . the city too indifferent, too proud, too unaware, too stupid even if one will, to enter any lists that involved her moving from her base and that thereby . . . enjoyed the enormous 'pull,' for making her impression, of ignoring everything but her own perversities and then of driving these home with an emphasis not to be gainsaid." The young American ("brooding monster that I was, born to discriminate À TOUT PROPOS") was soon breakfasting with the gentleman upstairs (Mr. Albert Rutson), eating his fried sole and marmalade with other gentlemen from the Home Office, the Foreign Office, the House of Commons, whose freedom to lounge over that meal impressed him greatly, and whose close questioning as to the composition of Grant's first Cabinet embarrassed him not a little. The whole scene, which it would be an impiety to dismember further, has the very breath of the age in it. The whiskers, the leisure, the intentness of those gentlemen upon politics, their conviction that the composition of Cabinets was the natural topic for the breakfast-table, and that a stranger unable, as Henry James found himself, to throw light upon it was "only not perfectly ridiculous because perfectly insignificant"-- all this provides a picture that many of us will be able to see again as we saw it once perhaps from the perch of an obliging pair of shoulders.

The main facts about that London, as all witnesses agree in testifying, were its smallness compared with our city, the limited number of distractions and amusements available, and the consequent tendency of all people worth knowing to know each other and to form a very accessible and, at the same time, highly enviable society. Whatever the quality that gained you admittance, whether it was that you had done something or showed yourself capable of doing something worthy of respect, the compliment was not an empty one. A young man coming up to London might in a few months claim to have met Tennyson, Browning, Matthew Arnold, Carlyle, Froude, George Eliot, Herbert Spencer, Huxley, and Mill. He had met them; he had not merely brushed against them in a crowd. He had heard them talk; he had even offered something of his own. The conditions of those days allowed a kind of conversation which, so the survivors always maintain, is an art unknown in what they are pleased to call our chaos. What with recurring dinner parties and Sunday calls, and country visits lasting far beyond the week-ends of our generation, the fabric of friendship was solidly built up and carefully preserved. The tendency perhaps was rather to a good fellowship in which the talk was wide-sweeping, extremely well informed, and impersonal than to the less formal, perhaps more intense and indiscriminate, intimacies of to-day. We read of little societies of the sixties, the Cosmopolitan and the Century, meeting on Wednesday and on Sunday evenings to discuss the serious questions of the times, and we have the feeling that they could claim a more representative character than anything of the sort we can show now. We are left with the impression that whatever went forward in those days, either among the statesmen or among the men of letters--and there was a closer connection than there is now--was promoted or inspired by the members of this group. Undoubtedly the resources of the day--and how magnificent they were!--were better organized; and it must occur to every reader of their memoirs that a reason is to be found in the simplicity which accepted the greatness of certain names and imposed something like order on their immediate neighbourhood. Having crowned their kin they worshipped him with the most whole-hearted loyalty. Groups of people would come together at Freshwater, in that old garden where the houses of Melbury Road now stand, or in various London centres, and live as it seems to us for months at a time, some of them indeed for the duration of their lives, in the mood of the presiding genius. Watts and Burne-Jones in one quarter of the town, Carlyle in another, George Eliot in a third, almost as much as Tennyson in his island, imposed their laws upon a circle which had spirit and beauty to recommend it as well as an uncritical devotion.

Henry James, of course, was not a person to accept laws or to make one of any circle in a sense which implies the blunting of the critical powers. Happily for us, he came over not only with the hoarded curiosity of years, but also with the detachment of the stranger and the critical sense of the artist. He was immensely appreciative, but he was also immensely observant. Thus it comes about that his fragment revives, indeed stamps afresh, the great figures of the epoch, and, what is no less important, illumines the lesser figures by whom they were surrounded. Nothing could be happier than his portrait of Mrs. Greville, "with her exquisite good nature and her innocent fatuity," who was, of course, very much an individual, but also a type of the enthusiastic sisterhood which, with all its extravagances and generosities and what we might unkindly, but not without the authority of Henry

James, call absurdity, now seems extinct. We shall not spoil the reader's impression of the superb passage describing a visit arranged by Mrs. Greville to George Eliot by revealing what happened on that almost tragic occasion. It is more excusable to dwell for a moment upon the drawing-room at Milford Cottage,

the most embowered retreat for social innocence that it was possible to conceive. . . . The red candles in the red shades have remained with me, inexplicably, as a vivid note of this pitch, shedding their rosy light, with the autumn gale, the averted reality, all shut out, upon such felicities of feminine helplessness as I couldn't have prefigured in advance, and as exemplified, for further gathering in, the possibilities of the old tone.

The drawn curtains, the "copious service," the second volume of the new novel "half-uncut" laid ready to hand, "the exquisite head and incomparable brush of the domesticated collie"--that is the familiar setting. He recalls the high-handed manner in which these ladies took their way through life, baffling the very stroke of age and disaster with their unquenchable optimism, ladling out with both hands every sort of gift upon their passage, and bringing to port in their tow the most incongruous and battered of derelicts. No doubt "a number of the sharp truths that one might privately apprehend beat themselves beautifully in vain" against such defences. Truth, so it seems to us, was not so much disregarded as flattered out of countenance by the energy with which they pursued the beautiful, the noble, the poetic, and ignored the possibility of another side of things. The extravagant steps which they would take to snare whatever grace or atmosphere they desired at the moment lend their lives in retrospect a glamour of adventure, aspiration, and triumph such as seems for good or for evil banished from our conscious and much more critical day. Was a friend ill? A wall would be knocked down to admit the morning sun. Did the doctor prescribe fresh milk? The only perfectly healthy cow in England was at your service. All this personal exuberance Henry James brings back in the figure of Mrs. Greville, "friend of the super-eminent" and priestess at the different altars. Cannot we almost hear the "pleasant growling note of Tennyson" answering her "mild extravagance of homage" with "Oh, yes, you may do what you like---so long as you don't kiss me before the cabman!"

And then with the entrance of Lady Waterford, Henry James ponders lovingly the quality which seems to hang about those days and people as the very scent of the flower--"the quality of personal beauty, to say nothing of personal accomplishment as our fathers were appointed to enjoy it. . . . Scarce to be sated that form of wonder, to my own imagination I confess." Were they as beautiful as we like to remember them, or was it that the whole atmosphere made a beautiful presence, any sort of distinction or eminence indeed, felt in a way no longer so carefully arranged for, or so unquestionably accepted? Was it not all a part of the empty London streets, of the four-wheelers even, lined with straw, of the stuffy little boxes of the public dining rooms, of the protectedness, of the leisure? But if they had merely to stand and be looked at, how splendidly they did it! A certain width of space seems to be a necessary condition for the blooming of such splendid plants as Lady Waterford, who, when she had dazzled sufficiently with her beauty and presence, had only to take up her brush to be acclaimed the equal of Titian or of Watts.

Personality, whatever one may mean by it, seems to have been accorded a licence for the expression of itself for which we can find no parallel in the present day. The gift if you had it was encouraged and sheltered beyond the bounds of what now seems possible. Tennyson, of course, is the supreme example of what we mean, and happily for us Henry James was duly taken to that shrine and gives with extraordinary skill a new version of the mystery which in our case will supersede the old. "The fond prefigurements of youthful piety are predestined, more often than not, I think, experience interfering, to strange and violent shocks. . . . Fine, fine, fine, could he only be. . . ." So he begins, and so continuing for some time leads us up to the pronouncement that "Tennyson was not Tennysonian." The air one breathed at Aldworth was one in which nothing but "the blest obvious, or at least the blest outright, could so much as attempt to live . . . . It was a large and simple and almost empty occasion . . . . He struck me in truth as neither knowing nor communicating knowledge." He recited LOCKSLEY HALL and "Oh dear, oh dear. . . . I heard him in cool surprise take even more out of his verse than he had put in." And so by a series of qualifications which are all beautifully adapted to sharpen the image without in the least destroying it, we are led to the satisfactory and convincing conclusion, "My critical reaction hadn't in the least invalidated our great man's being a Bard--it had in fact made him and left him more a Bard than ever." We see, really for the first time, how obvious and simple and almost empty it was, how "the glory was without history," the poetic character "more worn than paid for, or at least more saved than spent," and yet somehow the great man revives and flourishes in the new conditions and dawns upon us more of a Bard than we had got into the habit of thinking him. The same service of defining, limiting, and restoring to life he performs as beautifully for the ghost of George Eliot, and proclaims himself, as the faithful will be glad to hear, "even a very Derondist of Derondists."

And thus looking back into the past which is all changed and gone (he could mark, he said, the very hour or the change) Henry James performs a last act of piety which is supremely characteristic of him. The English world of that day was very clear to him; it had a fineness and a distinction which he professed half humorously not to find in our "vast monotonous mob." It had given him friendship and opportunity and much else, no doubt, that it had no consciousness of giving. Such a gift he of all people could never forget; and this book of memories sounds to us like a superb act of thanksgiving. What could he do to make up for it all, he seems to have asked himself. And then with all the creative power at his command he summons back the past and makes us a present of that. If we could have had the choice, that is what we should have chosen, not entirely for what it gives us of the dead, but also for what it gives us of him. Many will hear his voice again in these pages; they will perceive once more that solicitude for others, that immense desire to help which had its origin, one might guess, in the aloofness and loneliness of the artist's life. It seemed as if he were grateful for the chance of taking part in the ordinary affairs of the world, of assuring himself that, in spite of his absorption with the fine and remote things of the imagination, he had not lost touch with human interests. To acknowledge any claim that was in the least connected with the friends or memories of the past gave him, for this reason, a peculiar joy; and we can believe that if he could have chosen, his last words would have been like these, words of recollection and of love.

HENRY JAMES

3. THE LETTERS OF HENRY JAMES
(* Written in 1920.)

Who, on stepping from the cathedral dusk, the growl and boom of the organ still in the ears, and the eyes still shaded to observe better whatever intricacy of carving or richness of marble may there be concealed, can breast the stir of the street and instantly and briskly sum up and deliver his impressions? How discriminate, how formulate? How, Henry James may be heard grimly asking, dare you pronounce any opinion whatever upon me? In the first place only by taking cover under some such figure as implies that, still dazed and well-nigh drowned, our gesture at the finish is more one of exclamation than of interpretation. To soothe and to inspirit there comes, a moment later, the consciousness that, although in the eyes of Henry James our attempt is foredoomed to failure, nevertheless his blessing is upon it. Renewal of life, on such terms as we can grant it, upon lips, in minds, here in London, here among English men and women, would receive from him the most generous acknowledgment; and with a royal complacency, he would admit that our activities could hardly be better employed. Nor are we left to grope without a guide. It would not be easy to find a difficult task better fulfilled than by Mr. Percy Lubbock in his introduction and connecting pararaphs. (* THE LETTERS OF HENRY JAMES. Edited by Percy Lubbock.) It seems to us, and this not only before reading the letters but more emphatically afterwards, that the lines of interpretation he lays down are the true ones. They end--as he is the first to declare--in the heart of darkness; but any understanding that we may have won of a difficult problem is at every point fortified and corrected by the help of his singularly thoughtful and intimate essay. His intervention is always illuminating.

It must be admitted that these remarks scarcely seem called for by anything specially abstruse in the first few chapters. If ever a young American proved himself capable of giving a clear and composed account of his experiences in Europe during the seventies of the last century that young American was Henry James. He recounts his seeings and doings, his dinings out and meetings, his country house visits, like a guest too well-bred to show surprise even if he feels it. A "cosmopolitanized American," as he calls himself, was far more likely, it appears, to find things flat than to find them surprising; to sink into the depths of English civilization as if it were a soft feather bed inducing sleep and warmth and security rather than shocks and sensations. Henry James, of course, was much too busy recording impressions to fall asleep; it only appears that he never did anything, and never met anyone, in those early days, capable of rousing him beyond the gay and sprightly mood so easily and amusingly sustained in his letters home. Yet he went everywhere; he met everyone, as the sprinkling of famous names and great occasions abundantly testify. Let one fair specimen suffice:

Yesterday I dined with Lord Houghton--with Gladstone,

Tennyson, Dr. Schliemann (the excavator of old Mycenae, &c.), and half a dozen other men of "high culture." I sat next but one to the Bard and heard most of his talk, which was all about port wine and tobacco; he seems to know much about them, and can drink a whole bottle of port at a sitting with no incommodity. He is very swarthy and scraggy, and strikes one' at first as much less handsome than his photos: but gradually you see that it's a face of genius. He had I know not what simplicity, speaks with a strange rustic accent and seemed altogether like a creature of some primordial English stock, a thousand miles away from American manufacture. Behold me after dinner conversing affably with Mr. Gladstone-not by my own seeking, but by the almost importunate affection of Lord H. But I was glad of a chance to feel the "personality" of a great political leader--or as G. is now thought here even, I think, by his partisans, ex-leader. That of Gladstone is very fascinating--his urbanity extreme-his eye that of a man of genius--and his apparent self-surrender to what he is talking of without a flaw. He made a great impression on me--greater than anyone I have seen here: though 'tis perhaps owing to my NAÏVETÉ, and unfamiliarity with statesmen....

And so to the Oxford and Cambridge boat-race. The impression is well and brightly conveyed; what we miss, perhaps, is any body of resistance to the impression--any warrant for thinking that the receiving mind is other than a stretched white sheet. The best comment upon that comes in his own words a few pages later. "It is something to have learned how to write." If we look upon many of these early pages as experiments in the art of writing by one whose standard of taste exacts that small things must be done perfectly before big things are even attempted, we shall understand that their perfection is of the inexpressive kind that often precedes a late maturity. He is saying all that his means allow him to say. Moreover, he is saying it already, as most good letter writers learn to say it, not to an individual but to a chosen assembly. "It is, indeed, I think, the very essence of a good letter to be shown," he wrote; "it is wasted if it is kept for ONE.... I give you full leave to read mine aloud at your soirees!" Therefore, if we refrain from quotation, it is not that passages of the necessary quality are lacking. It is, rather, that while he writes charmingly, intelligently and adequately of this, that and the other, we begin by guessing and end by resenting the fact that his mind is elsewhere. It is not the dinner parties--a hundred and seven in one season--nor the ladies and gentlemen, nor even the Tennysons and the Gladstones that interest him primarily; the pageant passes before him: the impressions ceaselessly descend; and yet as we watch we also wait for the clue, the secret of it all. It is, indeed, clear that if he discharged the duties of his position with every appearance of equanimity the choice of the position itself was one of momentous importance, constantly requiring examination, and, with its promise of different possibilities, harassing his peace till the end of time. On what spot of the civilized globe was he to settle? His vibrations and vacillations in front of that problem suffer much in our report of them, but in the early days the case against America was simply that ". . . it takes an old civilization to set a novelist in motion."

Next, Italy presented herself; but the seductions of "the golden climate" were fatal to work. Paris had obvious advantages, but the drawbacks were equally positive--"I have seen almost nothing of the literary fraternity, and there are fifty reasons why I should not become intimate with them. I don't like their wares, and they don't like any others; and, besides, they are not ACCUEILLANTS." London exercised a continuous double pressure of attraction and repulsion to which finally he succumbed, to the extent of making his headquarters in the metropolis without shutting his eyes to her faults. "I am attracted to London in spite of the long list of reasons why I should not be; I think it, on the whole, the best point of view in the world. . . . But the question is interminable." When he wrote that, he was thirty-seven; a mature age; an age at which the native growing confidently in his own soil is already putting forth whatever flower fate ordains and natural conditions allow. But Henry James had neither roots nor soil; he was of the tribe of wanderers and aliens; a winged visitant, ceaselessly circling and seeking, unattached, uncommitted, ranging hither and thither at his own free will, and only at length precariously settling and delicately inserting his proboscis in the thickset lusty blossoms of the old garden beds.

Here, then, we distinguish one of the strains, always to some extent present in the letters before us, from which they draw their unlikeness to any others in the language, and, indeed, bring us at times to doubt whether they are "in the language" at all. If London is primarily a point of view, if the whole field of human activity is only a prospect and a pageant, then we cannot help asking, as the store of impressions heaps itself up, what is the aim of the spectator, what is the purpose of his hoard? A spectator, alert, aloof, endlessly interested, endlessly observant, Henry James undoubtedly was; but as obviously, though not so simply, the long drawn process_ of adjustment and preparation was from first to last controlled and manipulated by a purpose which, as the years went by, only dealt more powerfully and completely with the treasures of a more complex sensibility. Yet, when we look to find the purpose expressed, to see the material in the act of transmutation, we are met by silence, we are blindly waved outside. "To write a series of good little tales I deem ample work for a life time. It's at least a relief to have arranged one's life time."The words are youthful, perhaps intentionally light but few and frail as they are, they have almost alone to bear the burden built upon them, to answer the questions and quiet the suspicions of those who insist that a writer must have a mission and proclaim it aloud. Scarcely for a moment does Henry James talk of his writing; never for an instant is the thought of it absent from his mind. Thus, in the letters to Stevenson abroad we hear behind everything else a brooding murmur of amazement and horror at the notion of living with savages. How, he seems to be asking himself, while on the surface all is admiration and affection, can he endure it--how could I write my books if I lived in Samoa with savages? All refers to his writing; all points in to that preoccupation. But so far as actual statement goes the books might have sprung as silently and spontaneously as daffodils in spring. No notice is taken of their birth. Nor does it matter to him what people say. Their remarks are probably wide of the point, or if they have a passing truth they are uttered in unavoidable ignorance of the fact that each book is a step onward in a gradual process of evolution, the plan of which is onward only to the author himself. He remains inscrutable. silent, and assured.

How, then, are we to explain the apparent inconsistency of his disappointment when, some years later, the failure of THE BOSTONIANS and PRINCESS CASAMASSIMA brought him face to face with the fact that he was not destined to be a popular novelist--

. . . I am still staggering [he wrote] a good deal under the mysterious and to me inexplicable injury wrought- -apparently--upon my situation by my two last novels, the BOSTONIANS and the PRINCESS, from which I expected so much and derived so little. They have reduced the desire, and the demand, for my productions to zero--as I judge from the fact that though I have for a good while past been writing a number of good short things, I remain irremediably unpublished.

Compensations at once suggested themselves; he was "really in better form then ever" and found himself "holding the 'critical world' at large in singular contempt" but we have Mr. Lubbock's authority for supposing that it was chiefly a desire to retrieve the failure of the novels that led him to strive so strenuously, and in the end so disastrously, for success upon the stage. Success and failure upon the lips of a man who never for a moment doubted the authenticity of his genius or for a second lowered his standard of the artist's duty have not their ordinary meaning. Perhaps we may hold that failure in the sense that Henry James used it meant, more than anything, failure on the part of the public to receive. That was the public's fault, but that did not lessen the catastrophe or make less desirable the vision of an order of things where the public gratefully and with understanding accepts at the artists' hands what is, after all, the finest essence, transmuted and returned, of the public itself. When GUY DOMVILLE failed, and Henry James for one "abominable quarter of an hour" faced the "yelling barbarians" and "learned what could be the savagery of their disappointment that one wasn't perfectly the SAME as everything else they had ever seen" he had no doubt of his genius; but he went home to reflect:

I have felt for a long time past that I have fallen upon evil days--every sign and symbol of one's being in the least wanted, anywhere or by anyone, having so utterly failed. A new generation, that I know not, and mainly prize not, has taken universal possession.

The public henceforward appeared to him, so far as it appeared at all, a barbarian crowd incapable of taking in their rude paws the beauty and delicacy that he had to offer. More and more was he confirmed in his conviction that an artist can neither live with the public, write for it, nor seek his material in the midst of it. A select group, representative of

191

civilization, had at the same time protested its devotion, but how far can one write for a select group? Is not genius itself restricted, or at least influenced in its very essence by the consciousness that its gifts are to the few, its concern with the few, and its revelation apparent only to scattered enthusiasts who may be the advance guard of the future or only a little band strayed from the high road and doomed to extinction while civilization marches irresistibly elsewhere? All this Henry James poised, pondered, and held in debate. No doubt the influence upon the direction of his work was profound. But for all that he went serenely forward; bought a house, bought a typewriter, shut himself up, surrounded himself with furniture of the right period, and was able at the critical moment by the timely, though rash, expenditure of a little capital to ensure that certain hideous new cottages did not deface his point of view. One admits to a momentary malice. The seclusion is so deliberate; the exclusion so complete. All within the sanctuary is so prosperous and smooth. No private responsibilities harassed him; no public duties claimed him; his health was excellent and his income, in spite of his protests to the contrary, more than adequate to his needs. The voice that issued from the hermitage might well speak calmly, subtly, of exquisite emotions, and yet now and then we are warned by something exacting and even acid in its tone that the effects of seclusion are not altogether benign. "Yes. Ibsen is ugly, common, hard, prosaic, bottomlessly bourgeois . . ." "But, oh, yes, dear Louis, [TESS OF THE D'URBERVILLES] is vile. The pretence of 'sexuality' is only equalled by the absence of it, and the abomination of the language by the author's reputation for style." The lack of "aesthetic curiosity" in Meredith and his circle was highly to be deplored. The artist in him "was nothing to the good citizen and liberalized bourgeois." The works of Tolstoy and Dostoevsky are "fluid puddings" and "when you ask me if I don't feel Dostoevsky's 'mad jumble, that flings things down in a heap,' nearer truth and beauty than the picking up and composing that you instance in Stevenson, I reply with emphasis that I feel nothing of the sort." It is true that in order to keep these points at their sharpest one has had to brush aside a mass of qualification and explanation which make each the apex of a formidable body of criticism. It is only for a moment that the seclusion seems cloistered, and the feelings of an artist confounded with those of a dilettante.

Yet as that second flits across the mind, with the chill of a shadow brushing the waves, we realize what a catastrophe for all of us it would have been if the prolonged experiment, the struggle and the solitude of Henry James's life had ended in failure. Excuses could have been found both for him and for us. It is impossible, one might have said, for the artist not to compromise, or, if he persists in his allegiance, then, almost inevitably, he must live apart, for ever alien, slowly perishing in his isolation. The history of literature is strewn with examples of both disasters. When, therefore, almost perceptibly at a given moment, late in the story, something yields, something is overcome, something dark and dense glows in splendour, it is as if the beacon flamed bright on the hilltop; as if before our eyes the crown of long deferred completion and culmination swung slowly into place. Not columns but pages, and not pages but chapters, might be filled with comment and attempted analysis of this late and mighty flowering, this vindication, this crowded gathering together and superb welding into shape of all the separate strands, alien instincts, irreconcilable desires of the twofold nature. For, as we dimly perceive, here at last two warring forces have coalesced; here, by a prodigious efflort of concentration, the field of human activity is brought into fresh focus, revealing new horizons, new landmarks, and new lights upon it of right and wrong.

But it is for the reader at leisure to delve in the rich material of the later letters and build up from it the complex figure of the artist in his completeness. If we choose two passages---one upon conduct, the other upon the gift of a leather dressing case--to represent Henry James in his later mood we purposely brush aside a thousand others which have innumerable good claims to be put in their place.

If there be a wisdom in not feeling--to the last throb-- the great things that happen to us, it is a wisdom that I shall never either know or esteem. Let your soul live--it's the only life that isn't on the whole a sell. . . .

That [the dressing case] is the grand fact of the situation- -that is the tawny lion, portentous creature in my path. I can't get past him, I can't get round him, and on the other hand he stands glaring at me, refusing to give way and practically blocking all my future. I can't live with him, you see; because

I can't live UP to him. His claims, his pretensions, his dimensions, his assumptions and consumptions, above all the manner in which he causes every surrounding object (on my poor premises or within my poor range) to tell a dingy, or deplorable tale--all this makes him the very scourge of my life, the very blot on my scutcheon. He doesn't regild that rusty metal--he simply takes up an attitude of gorgeous swagger, straight in front of all the rust and the rubbish, which makes me look as if I had stolen SOMEBODY ELSE'S (regarnished BLASON) and were trying to palm it off as my own.... HE IS OUT OF THE PICTURE--out of MINE; and behold me condemned to live for ever with that canvas turned to the wall. Do you know what that means?

And so on and so on. There, portentous and prodigious, we hear unmistakably the voice of Henry James. There, to our thinking, we have exploded in our ears the report of his enormous, sustained, increasing, and overwhelming love of life. It issues from whatever tortuous channels and dark tunnels like a flood at its fullest. There is nothing too little, too large, too remote, too queer for it not to flow round, float off and make its own. Nothing in the end has chilled or repressed him; everything has fed and filled him; the saturation is complete. The labours of the morning might be elaborate and austere. There remained an irrepressible fund of vitality which the flying hand at midnight addressed fully and affectionately to friend after friend, each sentence, from the whole fling of his person to the last snap of his fingers, firmly fashioned and throwing out at its swiftest well nigh incredible felicities of phrase.

The only difficulty, perhaps, was to find an envelope that would contain the bulky product, or any reason, when two sheets were blackened, for not filling a third. Truly, Lamb House was no sanctuary, but rather a "small, crammed and wholly unlucrative hotel," and the hermit no meagre solitary but a tough and even stoical man of the world, English in his humour, Johnsonian in his sanity, who lived every second with insatiable gusto and in the flux and fury of his impressions obeyed his own injunction to remain "as solid and fixed and dense as you can." For to be as subtle as Henry James one must also be as robust; to enjoy his power of exquisite selection one must have "lived and loved and cursed and floundered and enjoyed and suffered," and, with the appetite of a giant, have swallowed the whole.

Yet, if he shared with magnanimity, if he enjoyed hugely, there remained something incommunicable, something reserved, as if in the last resort, it was not to us that he turned, nor from us that he received, nor into our hands that he placed his offerings. There they stand, the many books, products of "an inexhaustible sensibility," all with the final seal upon them of artistic form, which, as it imposes its stamp, sets apart the object thus consecrated and makes it no longer part of ourselves. In this impersonality the maker himself desired to share--"to take it," as he said, "wholly, exclusively with the pen (the style, the genius) and absolutely not at all with the person," to be "the mask without the face," the alien in our midst, the worker who when his work is done turns even from that and reserves his confidence for the solitary hour, like that at midnight when, alone on the threshold of creation, Henry James speaks aloud to himself "and the prospect clears and flushes, and my poor blest old genius pats me so admirably and lovingly on the back that I turn, I screw round, and bend my lips to passionately, in my gratitude, kiss its hands." So that is why, perhaps, as life swings and clangs, booms and reverberates, we have the sense of an altar of service, of sacrifice, to which, as we pass out, we bend the knee.

GEORGE MOORE

The only criticism worth having at present is that which is spoken, not written--spoken over wine-glasses and coffee-cups late at night, flashed out on the spur of the moment by people passing who have not time to finish their sentences, let alone consider the dues of editors or the feelings of friends. About living writers these talker's (it is one of their most engaging peculiarities) are always in violent disagreement. Take George Moore, for example. George Moore is the best living novelist--and the worst; writes the most beautiful prose of his time--and the feeblest; has a passion for literature which none of those dismal pundits, his contemporaries, shares; but how whimsical his judgments are, how ill-balanced, childish and egotistical, into the bargain! So they hammer the horseshoe out; so the sparks fly; and the worth of the criticism lies not so much in the accuracy of each blow as in the heat it engenders, the sense it kindles that the matter of George Moore and his works is of the highest importance, which, without waiting another instant, we must settle for ourselves.

Perhaps it is not accident only, but a vague recollection of dipping and dallying in ESTHER WATERS, EVELYN INNES, THE LAKE, which makes us take down in its new and stately form HAIL AND FAREWELL (Heinemann)--the two large volumes which George Moore has written openly and directly about himself. For all his novels are written, covertly and obliquely, about himself, so at least memory would persuade us, and it may help us to understand them if we steep ourselves in the pure waters which are elsewhere tinged with fictitious flavours. But are not all novels about the writer's self, we might ask? It is only as he sees people that we can see them; his fortunes colour and his oddities shape his vision until what we see is not the thing itself, but the thing seen and the seer inextricably mixed. There are degrees, however. The great novelist feels, sees, believes with such intensity of conviction that he hurls his belief outside himself and it flies off and lives an independent life of its own, becomes Natasha, Pierre, Levin, and is no longer Tolstoy. When, however, Mr. Moore creates a Natasha she may be charming, foolish, lovely, but her beauty, her folly, her charm are not hers, but Mr. Moore's. All her qualities refer to him. In other words, Mr. Moore is completely lacking in dramatic power. On the face of it, ESTHER WATERS has all the appearance of a great novel; it has sincerity, shapeliness, style; it has surpassing seriousness and integrity; but because Mr. Moore has not the strength to project Esther from himself its virtues collapse and fall about it like a tent with a broken pole. There it lies, this novel without a heroine, and what remains of it is George Moore himself, a ruin of lovely language and some exquisite descriptions of the Sussex downs. For the novelist who has no dramatic power, no fire of conviction within, leans upon nature for support; she lifts him up and enhances his mood without destroying it.

But the defects of a novelist may well be the glories of his brother the autobiographer, and we find, to our delight, that the very qualities which weaken Mr. Moore's novels are the making of his memoirs. This complex character, at once diffident and self-assertive, this sportsman who goes out shooting in ladies' high-heeled boots, this amateur jockey who loves literature beyond the apple of his eye, this amorist who is so innocent, this sensualist who is so ascetic, this complex and uneasy character, in short, with its lack of starch and pomp and humbug, its pliability and malice and shrewdness and incompetence, is made of too many incompatible elements to concentrate into the diamond of a great artist, and is better occupied in exploring its own vagaries than in explaining those of other people. For one thing, Mr. Moore is without that robust belief in himself which leads men to prophesy and create. Nobody was ever more diffident. As a little boy they told him that only an ugly old woman would marry him, and he has never got over it. "For it is difficult for me to believe any good of myself. Within the oftentimes bombastic and truculent appearance that I present to the world trembles a heart shy as a wren in the hedgerow or a mouse along the wainscoting." The least noise startles him, and the ordinary proceedings of mankind fill him with wonder and alarm. Their streets have so many names; their coats have so many buttons; the ordinary business of life is altogether beyond him. But with the timidity of the mouse he has also its gigantic boldness. This meek grey innocent creature runs right over the lion's paws. There is nothing that Mr. Moore will not say; by his own confession he ought to be excluded from every drawing-room in South Kensington.

If his friends forgive him it is only because to Mr. Moore all things are forgiven. Once when he was a child, "inspired by an uncontrollable desire to break the monotony of infancy," he threw all his clothes into a hawthorn tree and "ran naked in front of my nurse or governess screaming with delight at the embarrassment I was causing her." The habit has remained with him. He loves to take off his clothes and run screaming with delight at the fuss and blush and embarrassment which he is causing that dear old governess, the British Public. But the antics of Mr. Moore, though impish and impudent, are, after all, so amusing and so graceful that the governess, it is said, sometimes hides behind a tree to watch. That scream of his, that garrulous chuckle as of small birds chattering in a nest, is a merry sound; and then how melodiously he draws out his long notes when dusk descends and the stars rise! Always you will find him haunting the evening, when the downs are fading into waves of silver and the grey Irish fields are melting into the grey Irish hills. The storm never breaks over his head, the thunder never roars in his ears, the rain never drenches him. No; the worst that befalls him is that Teresa has not filled the Moderator lamp sufficiently full, so that the company which is dining in the garden under the apple tree must adjourn to the dining-room, where Mr. Osborne, Mr. Hughes, Mr. Longworth, Mr. Seumas O'Sullivan, Mr. Atkinson and Mr. Yeats are awaiting them.

And then in the dining-room, Mr. Moore sitting down and offering a cigar to his friends, takes up again the thread of that interminable discourse, which, if it lapses into the gulfs of reverie for a moment, begins anew wherever he finds a bench or chair to sit on or can link his arm in a friend's, or can find even some discreet sympathetic animal who will only occasionally lift a paw in silence. He talks incessantly about books and politics; of the vision that came to him in the Chelsea road; how Mr. Colville bred Belgian hares on the Sussex downs; about the death of his cat; the Roman Catholic religion; how dogma is the death of literature; how the names of poets determine their poetry; how Mr. Yeats is like a crow, and he himself has been forced to sit on the window sill in his pyjamas. One thing follows another; out of the, present flowers the past; it is as easy, inconsequent, melodious as the smoke of those fragrant cigars. But as one listens more attentively one perceives that while each topic floats up as easily as cigar smoke into the air, the blue wreaths have a strange fixity; they do not disperse, they unite; they build up the airy chambers of a lifetime, and as we listen in the Temple Gardens, in Ebury Street, in Paris, in Dublin to Mr. Moore talking, we explore from start to finish, from those earliest days in Ireland to these latest in London, the habitation of his soul.

But let us apply Mr. Moore's own test to Mr. Moore's own work. What interests him, he says, is not the three or four beautiful poems that a man may have written, but the mind that he brings into the world; and "by a mind I mean a new way of feeling and seeing." When the fierce tide of talk once more washes the battlements of Mr. Moore's achievement let us throw into mid-stream these remarks;

not one of his novels is a masterpiece; they are silken tents which have no poles; but he has brought a new mind into the world; he has given us a new way of feeling and seeing; he has devised--very painfully, for he is above all things painstaking, eking out a delicate gift laboriously--a means of liquidating the capricious and volatile essence of himself and decanting it in these memoirs; and that, whatever the degree, is triumph, achievement, immortality. If, further, we try to establish the degree we shall go on to say that no one so inveterately literary is among the great writers; literature has wound itself about him like a veil, forbidding him the free use of his limbs; the phrase comes to him before the emotion; but we must add that he is nevertheless a born writer, a man who detests meals, servants, ease, respectability or anything that gets between him and his art; who has kept his freedom when most of his contemporaries have long ago lost theirs; who is ashamed of nothing but of being ashamed; who says whatever he has it in his mind to say, and has taught himself an accent, a cadence, indeed a language, for saying it in which, though they are not English, but Irish, will give him his place among the lesser immortals of our tongue.

THE NOVELS OF E. M. FORSTER
I

There are many reasons which should prevent one from criticizing the work of contemporaries. Besides the obvious uneasiness--the fear of hurting feelings--there is too the difficulty of being just. Coming out one by one, their books seem like parts of a design which is slowly uncovered. Our appreciation may be intense, but our curiosity is even greater. Does the new fragment add anything to what went before? Does it carry out our theory of the author's talent, or must we alter our forecast? Such questions ruffle what should be the smooth surface of our criticism and make it full of argument and interrogation. With a novelist like Mr. Forster this is specially true, for he is in any case an author about whom there is considerable disagreement. There is something baffling and evasive in the very nature of his gifts. So, remembering that we are at best only building up a theory which may be knocked down in a year or two by Mr. Forster himself, let us take Mr. Forster's novels in the order in which they were written, and tentatively and cautiously try to make them yield us an answer.

The order in which they were written is indeed of some importance, for at the outset we see that Mr. Forster is extremely susceptible to the influence of time. He sees his people much at the mercy of those conditions which change with the years. He is acutely conscious of the bicycle and of the motor car; of the public school and of the university; of the suburb and of the city. The social historian will find his books full of illuminating information. In 1905 Lilia learned to bicycle, coasted down the High Street on Sunday evening, and fell off at the turn by the church. For this she was given a talking to by her brother-in-law which she remembered to her dying day. It is on Tuesday that the housemaid cleans out the drawing-room at Sawston. Old maids blow into their gloves when they take them off. Mr. Forster is a novelist, that is to say, who sees his people in close contact with their surroundings. And therefore the colour and constitution of the year 1905 affect him far more than any year in the calendar could affect the romantic Meredith or the poetic Hardy. But we discover as we turn the page that observation is not an end in itself; it is rather the goad, the gadfly driving Mr. Forster to provide a refuge from this misery, an escape from this meanness. Hence we arrive at that balance of forces which plays so large a part in the structure of Mr. Forster's novels. Sawston implies Italy; timidity, wildness; convention, freedom; unreality, reality. These are the villains and heroes of much of his writing. In WHERE ANGELS FEAR TO TREAD the disease, convention, and the remedy, nature, are provided if anything with too eager a simplicity, too simple an assurance, but with what a freshness, what a charm! Indeed it would not be excessive if we discovered in this slight first novel evidence of powers which only needed, one might hazard, a more generous diet to ripen into wealth and beauty. Twenty-two years might well have taken the sting from the satire and shifted the proportions of the whole. But, if that is to some extent true, the years have had no power to obliterate the fact that, though Mr. Forster may be sensitive to the bicycle and the duster, he is also the most persistent devotee of the soul. Beneath bicycles and dusters, Sawston and Italy, Philip, Harriet, and Miss Abbott, there always lies for him--it is this which makes him so tolerant a satirist--a burning core. It is the soul; it is reality; it is truth; it is poetry; it is love; it decks itself in many shapes, dresses itself in many disguises. But get at it he must; keep from it he cannot. Over brakes and byres, over drawing-room carpets and mahogany sideboards, he flies in pursuit. Naturally the spectacle is sometimes comic, often fatiguing; but there are moments--and his first novel provides several instances--when he lays his hands on the prize.

Yet, if we ask ourselves upon which occasions this happens and how, it will seem that those passages which are least didactic, least conscious of the pursuit of beauty, succeed best in achieving it. When he allows himself a holiday--some phrase like that comes to our lips; when he forgets the vision and frolics and sports with the fact; when, having planted the apostles of culture in their hotel, he creates airily, joyfully, spontaneously, Gino the dentist's son sitting in the cafe with his friends, or describes--it is a masterpiece of comedy--the performance of LUCIA DI LAMMERMOOR, it is then that we feel that his aim is achieved. Judging, therefore, on the evidence of this first book, with its fantasy, its penetration, its remarkable sense of design, we should have said that once Mr. Forster had acquired freedom, had passed beyond the boundaries of Sawston, he would stand firmly on his feet among the descendants of Jane Austen and Peacock. But the second novel, THE LONGEST JOURNEY, leaves us baffled and puzzled. The opposition is still the same: truth and untruth; Cambridge and Sawston; sincerity and sophistication. But everything is accentuated. He builds his Sawston of thicker bricks and destroys it with stronger blasts. The contrast between poetry and realism is much more precipitous. And now we see much more clearly to what a task his gifts commit him. We see that what might have been a passing mood is in truth a conviction. He believes that a novel must take sides in the human conflict. He sees beauty--none more keenly; but beauty imprisoned in a fortress of brick and mortar whence he must extricate her. Hence he is always constrained to build the cage--society in all its intricacy and triviality--before he can free the prisoner. The omnibus, the villa, the suburban residence, are an essential part of his design. They are required to imprison and impede the flying flame which is so remorselessly caged behind them. At the same time, as we read THE LONGEST JOURNEY we are aware of a mocking spirit of fantasy which flouts his seriousness. No one seizes more deftly the shades and shadows of the social comedy; no one more amusingly hits off the comedy of luncheon and tea party and a game of tennis at the rectory. His old maids, his clergy, are the most lifelike we have had since Jane Austen laid down the pen. But he has into the bargain what Jane Austen had not--the impulses of a poet. The neat surface is always being thrown into disarray by an outburst of lyric poetry. Again and again in THE LONGEST JOURNEY we are delighted by some exquisite description of the country; or some lovely sight--like that when Rickie and Stephen send the paper boats burning through the arch--is made visible to us forever. Here, then, is a difficult family of gifts to persuade to live in harmony together: satire and sympathy; fantasy and fact; poetry and a prim moral sense. No wonder that we are often aware of contrary currents that run counter to each other and prevent the book from bearing down upon us and overwhelming us with the authority of a masterpiece. Yet if there is one gift more essential to a novelist than another it is the power of combination--the single vision. The success of the masterpieces seems to lie not so much in their freedom from faults--indeed we tolerate the grossest errors in them all--but in the immense persuasiveness of a mind which has completely mastered its perspective.

II

We look then, as time goes on, for signs that Mr. Forster is committing himself; that he is allying himself to one of the two great camps to which most novelists belong. Speaking roughly, we may divide them into the preachers and the teachers, headed by Tolstoy and Dickens, on the one hand, and the pure artists, headed by Jane Austen and Turgenev, on the other. Mr. Forster, it seems, has a strong impulse to belong to both camps at once. He has many of the instincts and aptitudes of the pure artist (to adopt the old classification)--an exquisite prose style, an acute sense of comedy, a power of creating characters in a few strokes which live in an atmosphere of their own; but he is at the same time highly conscious of a message. Behind the rainbow of wit and sensibility there is a vision which he is determined that we shall see. But his vision is of a peculiar kind and his message of an elusive nature. He has not great interest in institutions. He has none of that wide social curiosity which marks the work of Mr. Wells. The divorce law and the poor law come in for little of his attention. His concern is with the private life; his message is addressed to the soul. "It is the private life that holds out the mirror to infinity; personal intercourse, and that alone, that ever hints at a personality beyond our daily vision." Our business is not to build in brick and mortar, but to draw together the seen and the unseen. We must learn to build the "rainbow bridge that should connect the prose in us with the passion. Without it we are meaningless fragments, half monks, half beasts." This belief that it is the private life that matters, that it is the soul that is eternal, runs through all his writing. It is the conflict between Sawston and Italy in WHERE ANGELS FEAR TO TREAD; between Rickie and Agnes in THE LONGEST JOURNEY; between Lucy and Cecil in A ROOM WITH A VIEW. It deepens, it becomes more insistent as time passes. It forces him on from the lighter and more whimsical short novels past that curious interlude, THE CELESTIAL OMNIBUS, to the two large books, HOWARDS END and A PASSAGE TO INDIA, which mark his prime.

But before we consider those two books let us look for a moment at the nature of the problem he sets himself. It is the soul that matters; and the soul, as we have seen, is caged in a solid villa of red brick somewhere in the suburbs of London. It seems, then, that if his books are to succeed in their mission his reality must at certain points become irradiated; his brick must be lit up; we must see the whole building saturated with light. We have at once to believe in the complete reality of the suburb and in the complete reality of the soul. In this combination of realism and mysticism his closest affinity is, perhaps, with Ibsen. Ibsen has the same realistic power. A room is to him a room, a writing table a writing table, and a waste-paper basket a waste-paper basket. At the same time, the paraphernalia of reality have at certain moments to become the veil through which we see infinity. When Ibsen achieves this, as he certainly does, it is not by performing some miraculous conjuring trick at the critical moment. He achieves it by putting us into the right mood from the very start and by giving us the right materials for his purpose. He gives us the effect of ordinary life, as Mr. Forster does, but he gives it us by choosing a very few facts and those of a highly relevant kind. Thus when the moment of illumination comes we accept it implicitly. We are neither roused nor puzzled; we do not have to ask ourselves, What does this mean? We feel simply that the thing we are looking at is lit up, and its depths revealed. It has not ceased to be itself by becoming something else.

Something of the same problem lies before Mr. Forster-- how to connect the actual thing with the meaning of the thing and to carry the reader's mind across the chasm which divides the two without spilling a single drop of its belief. At certain moments on the Arno, in Hertfordshire, in Surrey, beauty leaps from the scabbard, the fire of truth flames through the crusted earth; we must see the red brick villa in the suburbs of London lit up. But it is in these great scenes which are the justification of the huge elaboration of the realistic novel that we are most aware of failure. For it is here that Mr. Forster makes the change from realism to symbolism; here that the object which has been so uncompromisingly solid becomes, or should become, luminously transparent. He fails, one is tempted to think, chiefly because that admirable gift of his for observation has served him too well. He has recorded too much and too literally. He has given us an almost photographic picture on one side of the page; on the other he asks us to see the same view transformed and radiant with eternal fires. The bookcase which falls upon Leonard Bast in HOWARDS END should perhaps come down upon him with all the dead weight of smoke-dried culture; the Marabar caves should appear to us not real caves but, it may be, the soul of India. Miss Quested should be transformed from an English girl on a picnic to arrogant Europe straying into the heart of the East and getting lost there. We qualify these statements, for indeed we are not quite sure whether we have guessed aright. Instead of getting that sense of instant certainty which we get in THE WILD DUCK or in THE MASTER BUILDER, we are puzzled, worried. What does this mean? we ask ourselves. What ought we to understand by this? And the hesitation is fatal. For we doubt both things--the real and the symbolical: Mrs. Moore, the nice old lady, and Mrs. Moore, the sibyl. The conjunction of these two different realities seems to cast doubt upon them both. Hence it is that there is so often an ambiguity at the heart of Mr. Forster's novels. We feel that something has failed us at the critical moment; and instead of seeing, as we do in THE MASTER BUILDER, one single whole we see two separate parts.

The stories collected under the title of THE CELESTIAL OMNIBUS represent, it may be, an attempt on Mr. Forster's part to simplify the problem which so often troubles him of connecting the prose and poetry of life. Here he admits definitely if discreetly the possibility of magic. Omnibuses drive to Heaven; Pan is heard in the brushwood; girls turn into trees. The stories are extremely charming. They release the fantasticality which is laid under such heavy burdens in the novels. But the vein of fantasy is not deep enough or strong enough to fight single-handed against those other impulses which are part of his endowment. We feel that he is an uneasy truant in fairyland. Behind the hedge he always hears the motor horn and the shuffling feet of tired wayfarers, and soon he must return. One slim volume indeed contains all that he has allowed himself of pure fantasy. We pass from the freakish land where boys leap into the arms of Pan and girls become trees to the two Miss Schlegels, who have an income of six hundred pounds apiece and live in Wickham Place.

III

Much though we may regret the change, we cannot doubt that it was right. For none of the books before HOWARDS END and A PASSAGE TO INDIA altogether drew upon the full range of Mr. Forster's powers. With his queer and in some ways contradictory assortment of gifts, he needed, it seemed, some subject which would stimulate his highly sensitive and active intelligence, but would not demand the extremes of romance or passion; a subject which gave him material for criticism, and invited investigation; a subject which asked to be built up of an enormous number of slight yet precise observations, capable of being tested by an extremely honest yet sympathetic mind; yet, with all this, a subject which when finally constructed would show up against the torrents of the sunset and the eternities of night with a symbolical significance. In HOWARDS END the lower middle, the middle, the upper middle classes of English society are so built up into a complete fabric. It is an attempt on a larger scale than hitherto, and, if it fails, the size of the attempt is largely responsible. Indeed, as we think back over the many pages of this elaborate and highly skilful book, with its immense technical accomplishment, and also its penetration, its wisdom and its beauty, we may wonder in what mood of the moment we can have been prompted to call it a failure. By all the rules, still more by the keen interest with which we have read it from start to finish, we should have said success. The reason is suggested perhaps by the manner of one's praise. Elaboration, skill, wisdom, penetration, beauty--they are all there, but they lack fusion; they lack cohesion; the book as a whole lacks force. Schlegels, Wilcoxes, and Basts, with all that they stand for of class and environment, emerge with extraordinary verisimilitude, but the whole effect is less satisfying than that of the much slighter but beautifully harmonious WHERE ANGELS FEAR TO TREAD. Again we have the sense that there is some perversity in Mr. Forster's endowment so that his gifts in their variety and number tend to trip each other up. If he were less scrupulous, less just, less sensitively aware of the different aspects of every case, he could, we feel, come down with greater force on one precise point. As it is, the strength of his blow is dissipated. He is like a light sleeper who is always being woken by something in the room. The poet is twitched away by the satirist; the comedian is tapped on the shoulder by the moralist; he never loses himself or forgets himself for long in sheer delight in the beauty or the interest of things as they are. For this reason the lyrical passages in his books, often of great beauty in themselves, fail of their due effect in the context. Instead of flowering naturally--as in Proust, for instance--from an overflow of interest and beauty in the object itself, we feel that they have been called into existence by some irritation, are the effort of a mind outraged by ugliness to supplement it with a beauty which, because it originates in protest, has something a little febrile about it.

Yet in HOWARDS END there are, one feels, in solution all the qualities that are needed to make a masterpiece. The characters are extremely real to us. The ordering of the story is masterly. That indefinable but highly important thing, the atmosphere of the book, is alight with intelligence; not a speck of humbug, not an atom of falsity is allowed to settle. And again, but on a larger battlefield, the struggle goes forward which takes place in all Mr. Forster's novels-- the struggle between the things that matter and the things that do not matter, between reality and sham, between the truth and the lie. Again the comedy is exquisite and the observation faultless. But again, just as we are yielding ourselves to the pleasures of the imagination, a little jerk rouses us. We are tapped on the shoulder. We are to notice this, to take heed of that. Margaret or Helen, we are made to understand, is not speaking simply as herself; her words have another and a larger intention. So, exerting ourselves to find out the meaning, we step from the enchanted world of imagination, where our faculties work freely, to the twilight world of theory, where only our intellect functions dutifully. Such moments of disillusionment have the habit of coming when Mr. Forster is most in earnest, at the crisis of the book, where the sword falls or the bookcase drops. They bring, as we have noted already, a curious insubstantiality into the "great scenes" and the important figures. But they absent themselves entirely from the comedy. They make us wish, foolishly enough, to dispose Mr. Forster's gifts differently and to restrict him to write comedy only. For directly he ceases to feel responsible for his characters' behaviour, and forgets that he should solve the problem of the universe, he is the most diverting of novelists. The admirable Tibby and the exquisite Mrs. Munt in HOWARDS END, though thrown in largely to amuse us, bring a breath of fresh air in with them. They inspire us with the intoxicating belief that they are free to wander as far from their creator as they choose. Margaret, Helen, Leonard Bast, are closely tethered and vigilantly overlooked lest they may take matters into their own hands and upset the theory. But Tibby and Mrs. Munt go where they like, say what they like, do what they like. The lesser characters and the unimportant scenes in Mr. Forster's novels thus often remain more vivid than those with which, apparently, most pain has been taken. But it would be unjust to part from this big, serious, and highly interesting book without recognizing that it is an important if unsatisfactory piece of work which may well be the prelude to something as large but less anxious.

IV

Many years passed before A PASSAGE TO INDIA appeared. Those who hoped that in the interval Mr. Forster might have developed his technique so that it yielded rather more easily to the impress of his whimsical mind and gave freer outlet to the poetry and fantasy which play about in him were disappointed. The attitude is precisely the same four-square attitude which walks up to life as if it were a house with a front door, puts its hat on the table in the hall and proceeds to visit all the rooms in an orderly manner. The house is still the house of the British middle classes. But there is a change from HOWARDS END. Hitherto Mr. Forster has been apt to pervade his books like a careful hostess who is anxious to introduce, to explain, to warn her guests of a step here, of a draught there. But here, perhaps in some disillusionment both with his guests and with his house, he seems to have relaxed these cares. We are allowed to ramble over this extraordinary continent almost alone. We notice things, about the country especially, spontaneously, accidentally almost, as if we were actually there; and now it was the sparrows flying about the pictures that caught our eyes, now the elephant with the painted forehead, now the enormous but badly designed ranges of hills. The people too, particularly the Indians, have something of the same casual, inevitable quality. They are not perhaps quite so important as the land, but they are alive; they are sensitive. No longer do we feel, as we used to feel in England, that they will be allowed to go only so far and no further lest they may upset some theory of the author's. Aziz is a free agent. He is the most imaginative character that Mr. Forster has yet created, and recalls Gino the dentist in his first book, WHERE ANGELS FEAR TO TREAD. We may guess indeed that it has helped Mr. Forster to have put the ocean between him and Sawston. It is a relief, for a time, to be beyond the influence of Cambridge. Though it is still a necessity for him to build a model world which he can submit to delicate and precise criticism, the model is on a larger scale. The English society, with all its pettiness and its vulgarity and its streak of heroism, is set against a bigger and a more sinister background. And though it is still true that there are ambiguities in important places, moments of imperfect symbolism, a greater accumulation of facts than the imagination is able to deal with, it seems as if the double vision which troubled us in the earlier books was in process of becoming single. The saturation is much more thorough. Mr. Forster has almost achieved the great feat of animating this dense, compact body of observation with a spiritual light. The book shows signs of fatigue and disillusionment; but it has chapters of clear and triumphant beauty, and above all it makes us wonder, What will he write next?

MIDDLEBROW
(* This letter was written, but not sent to The New Statesman.)

To THE EDITOR OF THE "NEW STATESMAN"

Sir,

Will you allow me to draw your attention to the fact that in a review of a book by me (October) your reviewer omitted to use the word Highbrow? The review, save for that omission, gave me so much pleasure that I am driven to ask you, at the risk of appearing unduly egotistical, whether your reviewer, a man of obvious intelligence, intended to deny my claim to that title? I say "claim," for surely I may claim that title when a great critic, who is also a great novelist, a rare and enviable combination, always calls me a highbrow when he condescends to notice my work in a great newspaper; and, further, always finds space to inform not only myself, who know it already, but the whole British Empire, who hang on his words, that I live in Bloomsbury? Is your critic unaware of that fact too? Or does he, for all his intelligence, maintain that it is unnecessary in reviewing a book to add the postal address of the writer?

His answer to these questions, though of real value to me, is of no possible interest to the public at large. Of that I am well aware. But since larger issues are involved, since the Battle of the Brows troubles, I am told, the evening air, since the finest minds of our age have lately been engaged in debating, not without that passion which befits a noble cause, what a highbrow is and what a lowbrow, which is better and which is worse, may I take this opportunity to express my opinion and at the same time draw attention to certain aspects of the question which seem to me to have been unfortunately overlooked?

Now there can be no two opinions as to what a highbrow is. He is the man or woman of thoroughbred intelligence who rides his mind at a gallop across country in pursuit of an idea. That is why I have always been so proud to be called highbrow. That is why, if I could be more of a highbrow I would. I honour and respect highbrows. Some of my relations have been highbrows; and some, but by no means all, of my friends. To be a highbrow, a complete and representative highbrow, a highbrow like Shakespeare, Dickens, Byron, Shelley, Keats, Charlotte Brontë, Scott, Jane Austen, Flaubert, Hardy or Henry James--to name a few highbrows from the same profession chosen at random--is of course beyond the wildest dreams of my imagination. And, though I would cheerfully lay myself down in the dust and kiss the print of their feet, no person of sense will deny that this passionate preoccupation of theirs--riding across country in pursuit of ideas--often leads to disaster. Undoubtedly, they come fearful croppers. Take Shelley--what a mess he made of his life! And Byron, getting into bed with first one woman and then with another and dying in the mud at Missolonghi. Look at Keats, loving poetry and Fanny Brawne so intemperately that he pined and died of consumption at the age of twenty-six. Charlotte Brontë again--I have beep assured on good authority that Charlotte Brontë was, with the possible exception of Emily, the worst governess in the British Isles. Then there was Scott--he went bankrupt, and left, together with a few magnificent novels, one house, Abbotsford, which is perhaps the ugliest in the whole Empire. But surely these instances are enough--I need not further labour the point that highbrows, for some reason or another, are wholly incapable of dealing successfully with what is called real life. That is why, and here I come to a point that is often surprisingly ignored, they honour so wholeheartedly and depend so completely upon those who are called lowbrows. By a lowbrow is meant of course a man or a woman of thoroughbred vitality who rides his body in pursuit of a living at a gallop across life. That is why I honour and respect lowbrows--and I have never known a highbrow who did not. In so far as I am a highbrow (and my imperfections in that line are well known to me) I love lowbrows; I study them; I always sit next the conductor in an omnibus and try to get him to tell me what it is like--being a conductor. In whatever company I am I always try to know what it is like--being a conductor, being a woman with ten children and thirty-five shillings a week, being a stockbroker, being an admiral, being a bank clerk, being a dressmaker, being a duchess, being a miner, being a cook, being a prostitute. All that lowbrows do is of surpassing interest and wonder to me, because, in so far as I am a highbrow, I cannot do things myself.

This brings me to another point which is also surprisingly overlooked. Lowbrows need highbrows and honour them just as much as highbrows need lowbrows and honour them. This too is not a matter that requires much demonstration. You have only to stroll along the Strand on a wet winter's night and watch the crowds lining up to get into the movies. These lowbrows are waiting, after the day's work, in the rain, sometimes for hours, to get into the cheap seats and sit in hot theatres in order to see what their lives look like. Since they are lowbrows, engaged magnificently and adventurously in riding full tilt from one end of life to the other in pursuit of a living, they cannot see themselves doing it. Yet nothing interests them more. Nothing matters to them more. It is one of the prime necessities of life to them--to be shown what life looks like. And the highbrows, of course, are the only people who can show them. Since they are the only people who do not do things, they are the only people who can see things being done. This is so--and so it is I am certain; nevertheless we are told--the air buzzes with it by night, the press booms with it by day, the very donkeys in the fields do nothing but bray it, the very curs in the streets do nothing but bark it--"Highbrows hate lowbrows! Lowbrows hate highbrows!"--when highbrows need lowbrows, when lowbrows need highbrows, when they cannot exist apart, when one is the complement and other side of the other! How has such a lie come into existence? Who has set this malicious gossip afloat?

There can be no doubt about that either. It is the doing of the middlebrows. They are the people, I confess, that I seldom regard with entire cordiality. They are the go-betweens; they are the busy-bodies who run from one to the other with their tittle tattle and make all the mischief--the middlebrows, I repeat. But what, you may ask, is a middlebrow? And that, to tell the truth, is no easy question to answer. They are neither one thing nor the other. They are not highbrows, whose brows are high; nor lowbrows, whose brows are low. Their brows are betwixt and between. They do not live in Bloomsbury which is on high ground; nor in Chelsea, which is on low ground. Since they must live somewhere presumably, they live perhaps in South Kensington, which is betwixt and between. The middlebrow is the man, or woman, of middlebred intelligence who ambles and saunters now on this side of the hedge, now on that, in pursuit of no single object, neither art itself nor life itself, but both mixed indistinguishably, and rather nastily, with money, fame, power, or prestige. The middlebrow curries favour with both sides equally. He goes to the lowbrows and tells them that while he is not quite one of them, he is almost their friend. Next moment he rings up the highbrows and asks them with equal geniality whether he may not come to tea. Now there are highbrows--I myself have known duchesses who were highbrows, also charwomen, and they have both told me with that vigour of language which so often unites the aristocracy with the working classes, that they would rather sit in the coal cellar, together, than in the drawing-room with middlebrows and pour out tea. I have myself been asked-- but may I, for the sake of brevity, cast this scene which is only partly fictitious, into the form of fiction?--I myself, then, have been asked to come and "see" them--how strange a passion theirs is for being "seen"! They ring me up, therefore, at about eleven in the morning, and ask me to come to tea. I go to my wardrobe and consider, rather lugubriously, what is the right thing to wear? We highbrows may be smart, or we may be shabby; but we never have the right thing to wear. I proceed to ask next: What is the right thing to say? Which is the right knife to use? What is the right book to praise? All these are things I do not know for myself. We highbrows read what we like and do what we like and praise what we like. We also know what we dislike--for example, thin bread and butter tea. The difficulty of eating thin bread and butter in white kid gloves has always seemed to me one of life's more insuperable problems. Then I dislike bound volumes of the classics behind plate glass. Then I distrust people who call both Shakespeare and Wordsworth equally "Bill"--it is a habit moreover that leads to confusion. And in the matter of clothes, I like people either to dress very well; or to dress very badly; I dislike the correct thing in clothes. Then there is the question of games. Being a highbrow I do not play them. But I love watching people play who have a passion for games. These middlebrows pat balls about; they poke their bats and muff their catches at cricket. And when poor Middlebrow mounts on horseback and that animal breaks into a canter, to me there is no sadder sight in all Rotten Row. To put it in a nutshell (in order to get on with the story) that tea party was not wholly a success, nor altogether a failure; for Middlebrow, who writes, following me to the door, clapped me briskly on the back, and said "I'm sending you my book!" (Or did he call it "stuff?") And his book comes--sure enough, though called, so symbolically, KEEPAWAY, [Keepaway is the name of a preparation used to distract the male dog from the female at certain seasons] it comes. And I read a page here, and I read a page there (I am breakfasting, as usual, in bed). And it is not well written; nor is it badly written. It is not proper, nor is it improper--in short it is betwixt and between. Now if there is any sort of book for which I have, perhaps, an imperfect sympathy, it is the betwixt and between. And so, though I suffer from the gout of a morning--but if one's ancestors for two or three centuries have tumbled into bed dead drunk one has deserved a touch of that malady--I rise. I dress. I proceed weakly to the window. I take that book in my swollen right hand and toss it gently over the hedge into the field. The hungry sheep--did I remember to say that this part of the story takes place in the country?--the hungry sheep look up but are not fed.

But to have done with fiction and its tendency to lapse into poetry--I will now report a perfectly prosaic conversation in words of one syllable. I often ask my friends the lowbrows, over our muffins and honey, why it is that while we, the highbrows, never buy a middlebrow book, or go to a middlebrow lecture, or read, unless we are paid for doing so, a middlebrow review, they, on the contrary, take these middlebrow activities so seriously? Why, I ask (not of course on the wireless), are you so damnably modest? Do you think that a description of your lives, as they are, is too sordid and too mean to be beautiful? Is that why you prefer the middlebrow version of what they have the impudence to call real humanity?--this mixture of geniality and sentiment stuck together with a sticky slime of calves-foot jelly? The truth, if you would only believe it, is much more beautiful than any lie. Then again, I continue, how can you let the middlebrows teach you how to write?--you, who write so beautifully when you write naturally, that I would give both my hands to write as you do--for which reason I never attempt it, but do my best to learn the art of writing as a highbrow should. And again, I press on, brandishing a muffin on the point of a tea spoon, how dare the middlebrows teach you how to read-- Shakespeare for instance? All you have to do is to read him. The Cambridge edition is both good and cheap. If you find HAMLET difficult, ask him to tea. He is a highbrow. Ask Ophelia to meet him. She is a lowbrow. Talk to them, as you talk to me, and you will know more about Shakespeare than all the middlebrows in the world can teach you--I do not think, by the way, from certain phrases that Shakespeare liked middlebrows, or Pope either.

To all this the lowbrows reply--but I cannot imitate their style of talking--that they consider themselves to be common people without education. It is very kind of the middlebrows to try to teach them culture. And after all, the lowbrows continue, middlebrows, like other people, have to make money. There must be money in teaching and in writing books about Shakespeare. We all have to earn our livings nowadays, my friends the lowbrows remind me. I quite agree.

Even those of us whose Aunts came a cropper riding in India and left them an annual income of four hundred and rfifty pounds, now reduced, thanks to the war and other luxuries, to little more than two hundred odd, even we have to do that. And we do it, too, by writing about anybody who seems amusing--enough has been written about Shakespeare--Shakespeare hardly pays. We highbrows, I agree, have to earn our livings; but when we have earned enough to live on, then we live. When the middlebrows, on the contrary, have earned enough to live on, they go on earning enough to buy--what are the things that middlebrows always buy? Queen Anne furniture (faked, but none the less expensive); first editions of dead writers, always the worst; pictures, or reproductions from pictures, by dead painters; houses in what is called "the Georgian style"--but never anything new, never a picture by a living painter, or a chair by a living carpenter, or books by living writers, for to buy living art requires living taste. And, as that kind of art and that kind of taste are what middlebrows call "highbrow," "Bloomsbury," poor middlebrow spends vast sums on sham antiques, and has to keep at it scribbling away, year in, year out, while we highbrows ring each other up, and are off for a day's jaunt into the country. That is the worst of course of living in a set--one likes being with one's friends.

Have I then made my point clear, sir, that the true battle in my opinion lies not between highbrow and lowbrow, but between highbrows and lowbrows joined together in blood brotherhood against the bloodless and pernicious pest who comes between? If the B.B.C. stood for anything but the

Betwixt and Between Company they would use their control of the air not to stir strife between brothers, but to broadcast the fact that highbrows and lowbrows must band together to exterminate a pest which is the bane of all thinking and living. It may be, to quote from your advertisement columns, that "terrifically sensitive" lady novelists overestimate the dampness and dinginess of this fungoid growth. But all I can say is that when, lapsing into that stream which people call, so oddly, consciousness, and gathering wool from the sheep that have been mentioned above, I ramble round my garden in the suburbs, middlebrow seems to me to be everywhere. "What's that?" I cry. "Middlebrow on the cabbages? Middlebrow infecting that poor old sheep? And what about the moon?" I look up and, behold, the moon is under eclipse. "Middlebrow at it again!" I exclaim. "Middlebrow obscuring, dulling, tarnishing and coarsening even the silver edge of Heaven's own scythe." (I "draw near to poetry," see advt.) And then my thoughts, as Freud assures us thoughts will do, rush (Middlebrow's saunter and simper, out of respect for the Censor) to sex, and I ask of the sea-gulls who are crying on desolate sea sands and of the farm hands who are coming home rather drunk to their wives, what will become of us, men and women, if Middlwbrow has his way with us, and there is only a middle sex but no husbands or wives? The next remark I address with the utmost humility to the Prime Minister. "What, sir," I demand, "will be the fate of the British Empire and of our Dominions Across the Seas if Middlebrows prevail? Will you not, sir, read a pronouncement of an authoritative nature from Broadcasting House?"

Such are the thoughts, such are the fancies that visit "cultured invalidish ladies with private means" (see advt.) when they stroll in their suburban gardens and look at the cabbages and at the red brick villas that have been built by middlebrows so that middlebrows may look at the view. Such are the thoughts "at once gay and tragic and deeply feminine" (see advt.) of one who has not yet "been driven out of Bloomsbury" (advt. again), a place where lowbrows and highbrows live happily together on equal terms and priests are not, nor priestesses, and, to be quite frank, the adjective "priestly" is neither often heard nor held in high esteem. Such are the thoughts of one who will stay in Bloomsbury until the Duke of Bedford, rightly concerned for the respectability of his squares, raises the rent so high that Bloomsbury is safe for middlebrows to live in. Then she will leave.

May I conclude, as I began, by thanking your reviewer for his very courteous and interesting review, but may I tell him that though he did not, for reasons best known to himself, call me a highbrow, there is no name in the world that I prefer? I ask nothing better than that all reviewers, for ever, and everywhere, should call me a highbrow. I will do my best to oblige them. If they like to add Bloomsbury, W.C.1, that is the correct postal address, and my telephone number is in the Directory. But if your reviewer, or any other reviewer, dares hint that I live in South Kensington, I will sue him for libel. If any human being, man, woman, dog, cat or half-crushed worm dares call me "middlebrow" I will take my pen

and stab him, dead. Yours etc.,
 Virginia Woolf.

THE ART OF BIOGRAPHY
I

The art of biography, we say---but at once go on to ask, is biography an art? The question is foolish perhaps, and ungenerous certainly, considering the keen pleasure that biographers have given us. But the question asks itself so often that there must be something behind it. There it is, whenever a new biography is opened, casting its shadow on the page; and there would seem to be something deadly in that shadow, for after all, of the multitude of lives that are written, how few survive!

But the reason for this high death rate, the biographer might argue, is that biography, compared with the arts of poetry and fiction, is a young art. Interest in our selves and in other people's selves is a late development of the human mind. Not until the eighteenth century in England did that curiosity express itself in writing the lives of private people. Only in the nineteenth century was biography fully grown and hugely prolific. If it is true that there have been only three great biographers--Johnson, Boswell, and Lockhart--the reason, he argues, is that the time was short; and his plea, that the art of biography has had but little time to establish itself and develop itself, is certainly borne out by the textbooks. Tempting as it is to explore the reason--why, that is, the self that writes a book of prose came into being so many centuries after the self that writes a poem, why Chaucer preceded Henry James--it is better to leave that insoluble question unasked, and so pass to his next reason for the lack of masterpieces. It is that the art of biography is the most restricted of all the arts. He has his proof ready to hand. Here it is in the preface in which Smith, who has written the life of Jones, takes this opportunity of thanking old friends who have lent letters, and "last but not least" Mrs. Jones, the widow, for that help "without which," as he puts it, "this biography could not have been written." Now the novelist, he points out, simply says in his foreword, "Every character in this book is fictitious." The novelist is free; the biographer is tied.

There, perhaps, we come within hailing distance of that very difficult, again perhaps insoluble, question: What do we mean by calling a book a work of art? At any rate, here is a distinction between biography and fiction--a proof that they differ in the very stuff of which they are made. One is made with the help of friends, of facts; the other is created without any restrictions save those that the artist, for reasons that seem good to him, chooses to obey. That is a distinction; and there is good reason to think that in the past biographers have found it not. only a distinction but a very cruel distinction.

The widow and the friends were hard taskmasters. Suppose, for example, that the man of genius was immoral, ill-tempered, and threw the boots at the maid's head. The widow would say, "Still I loved him--he was the father of my children; and the public, who love his books, must on no account be disillusioned. Cover up; omit." The biographer obeyed. And thus the majority of Victorian biographies are

like the wax figures now preserved in Westminster Abbey, that were carried in funeral processions through the street-
-effigies that have only a smooth superficial likeness to the body in the coffin.

Then, towards the end of the nineteenth century, there was a change. Again for reasons not easy to discover, widows became broader-minded, the public keener-sighted; the effigy no longer carried conviction or satisfied curiosity. The biographer certainly won a measure of freedom. At least he could hint that there were scars and furrows on the dead man's face. Froude's Carlyle is by no means a wax mask painted rosy red. And following Froude there was Sir Edmund Gosse, who dared to say that his own father was a fallible human being. And following Edmund Gosse in the early years of the present century came Lytton Strachey.

II

The figure of Lytton Strachey is so important a figure in the history of biography, that it compels a pause. For his three famous books, EMINENT VICTORIANS, QUEEN VICTORIA, and ELIZABETH AND ESSEX, are of a stature to show both what biography can do and what biography cannot do. Thus they suggest many possible answers to the question whether biography is an art, and if not why it fails. Lytton Strachey came to birth as an author at a lucky moment. In 1918, when he made his first attempt, biography, with its new liberties, was a form that offered great attractions. To a writer like himself, who had wished to write poetry or plays but was doubtful of his creative power, biography seemed to offer a promising alternative. For at last it was possible to tell the truth about the dead; and the Victorian age was rich in remarkable figures many of whom had been grossly deformed by the effigies that had been plastered over them. To recreate them, to show them as they really were, was a task that called for gifts analogous to the poet's or the novelist's, yet did not ask that inventive power in which he found himself lacking.

It was well worth trying. And the anger and the interest that his short studies of Eminent Victorians aroused showed that he was able to make Manning, Florence Nightingale, Gordon, and the rest live as they had not lived since they were actually in the flesh. Once more they were the centre of a buzz of discussion. Did Gordon really drink, or was that an invention? Had Florence Nightingale received the Order of Merit in her bedroom or in her sitting room? He stirred the public, even though a European war was raging, to an astonishing interest in such minute matters. Anger and laughter mixed; and editions multiplied.

But these were short studies with something of the over-emphasis and the foreshortening of caricatures. In the lives of the two great Queens, Elizabeth and Victoria, he attempted a far more ambitious task. Biography had never had a fairer chance of showing what it could do. For it was now being put to the test by a writer who was capable of making use of all the liberties that biography had won: he was fearless; he had proved his brilliance; and he had learned his job. The result throws great light upon the nature of biography. For who can doubt after reading the two books again, one after the other, that the Victoria is a triumphant success, and that the ELIZABETH by comparison is a failure? But it seems too, as we compare them, that it was not Lytton Strachey who failed; it was the art of biography. In the VICTORIA he treated biography as a craft; he submitted to its limitations. In the ELIZABETH he treated biography as an art; he flouted its limitations.

But we must go on to ask how we have come to this conclusion and what reasons support it. In the first place it is clear that the two Queens present very different problems to their biographer. About Queen Victoria everything was known. Everything she did, almost everything she thought, was a matter of common knowledge. No one has ever been more closely verified and exactly authenticated than Queen Victoria. The biographer could not invent her, because at every moment some document was at hand to check his invention. And, in writing of Victoria, Lytton Strachey submitted to the conditions. He used to the full the biographer's power of selection and relation, but he kept strictly within the world of fact. Every statement was verified; every fact was authenticated. And the result is a life which, very possibly, will do for the old Queen what Boswell did for the old dictionary maker. In time to come Lytton Strachey's Queen Victoria will be Queen Victoria, just as Boswell's Johnson is now Dr. Johnson. The other versions will fade and disappear. It was a prodigious feat, and no doubt, having accomplished it, the author was anxious to press further. There was Queen Victoria, solid, real, palpable. But undoubtedly she was limited. Could not biography produce something of the intensity of poetry, something of the excitement of drama, and yet keep also the peculiar virtue that belongs to fact--its suggestive reality, its own proper creativeness?

Queen Elizabeth seemed to lend herself perfectly to the experiment. Very little was known about her. The society in which she lived was so remote that the habits, the motives, and even the actions of the people--of that age were full of strangeness and obscurity. "By what art are we to worm our way into those strange spirits? those even stranger bodies? The more clearly we perceive it, the more remote that singular universe becomes," Lytton Strachey remarked on one of the first pages. Yet there was evidently a "tragic history" lying dormant, half revealed, half concealed, in the story of the Queen and Essex. Everything seemed to lend itself to the making of a book that combined the advantages of both worlds, that gave the artist freedom to invent, but helped his invention with the support of facts--a book that was not only a biography but also a work of art.

Nevertheless, the combination proved unworkable; fact and fiction refused to mix. Elizabeth never became real in the sense that Queen Victoria had been real, yet she never became fictitious in the sense that Cleopatra or Falstaff is fictitious. The reason would seem to be that very little was known--he was urged to invent; yet something was known--his invention was checked. The Queen thus moves in an ambiguous world, between fact and fiction, neither embodied nor disembodied. There is a sense of vacancy and effort, of a tragedy that has no crisis, of characters that meet but do not clash.

If this diagnosis is true we are forced to say that the trouble lies with biography itself. It imposes conditions, and those conditions are that it must be based upon fact. And by fact in biography we mean facts that can be verified by other people besides the artist. If he invents facts as an artist invents them--facts that no one else can verify--and tries to combine them with facts of the other sort, they destroy each other.

Lytton Strachey himself seems in the QUEEN VICTORIA to have realized the necessity of this condition, and to have yielded to it instinctively. "The first forty-two years of the Queen's life," he wrote, "are illuminated by a great and varied quantity of authentic information. With Albert's death a veil descends." And when with Albert's death the veil descended and authentic information failed, he knew that the biographer must follow suit. "We must be content with a brief and summary relation," he wrote; and the last years are briefly disposed of. But the whole of Elizabeth's life was lived behind a far thicker veil than the last years of Victoria. And yet, ignoring his own admission, he went on to write, not a brief and summary relation, but a whole book about those strange spirits and even stranger bodies of whom authentic information was lacking. On his own showing, the attempt was doomed to failure.

III

It seems, then, that when the biographer complained that he was tied by friends, letters, and documents he was laying his finger upon a necessary element in biography; and that it is also a necessary limitation. For the invented character lives in a free world where the facts are verified by one person only--the artist himself. Their authenticity lies in the truth of his own vision. The world created by that vision is rarer, intenser, and more wholly of a piece than the world that is largely made of authentic information supplied by other people. And because of this difference the two kinds of fact will not mix; if they touch they destroy each other. No one, the conclusion seems to be, can make the best of both worlds; you must choose, and you must abide by your choice.

But though the failure of ELIZABETH AND ESSEX leads to this conclusion, that failure, because it was the result of a daring experiment carried out with magnificent skill, leads the way to further discoveries. Had he lived, Lytton Strachey would no doubt himself have explored the vein that he had opened. As it is, he has shown us the way in which others may advance. The biographer is bound by facts--that is so; but, if it is so, he has the right to all the facts that are available. If Jones threw boots at the maid's head, had a mistress at Islington, or was found drunk in a ditch after a night's debauch, he must be free to say so--so far at least as the law of libel and human sentiment allow.

But these facts are not like the facts of science--once

they are discovered, always the same. They are subject to changes of opinion; opinions change as the times change. What was thought a sin is now known, by the light of facts won for us by the psychologists, to be perhaps a misfortune; perhaps a curiosity; perhaps neither one nor the other, but a trifling foible of no great importance one way or the other. The accent on sex has changed within living memory. This leads to the destruction of a great deal of dead matter still obscuring the true features of the human face. Many of the old chapter headings--life at college, marriage, career--are shown to be very arbitrary and artificial distinctions. The real current of the hero's existence took, very likely, a different course.

Thus the biographer must go ahead of the rest of us, like the miner's canary, testing the atmosphere, detecting falsity, unreality, and the presence of obsolete conventions. His sense of truth must he alive and on tiptoe. Then again, since we live in an age when a thousand cameras are pointed, by newspapers, letters, and diaries, at every character from every angle, he must be prepared to admit contradictory versions of the same face. Biography will enlarge its scope by hanging up looking glasses at odd corners. And yet from all this diversity it will bring out, not a riot of confusion, but a richer unity. And again, since so much is known that used to be unknown, the question now inevitably asks itself, whether the lives of great men only should be recorded. Is not anyone who has lived a life, and left a record of that life, worthy of biography--the failures as well as the successes, the humble as well as the illustrious? And what is greatness? And what smallness? We must revise our standards of merit and set up new heroes for our admiration.

IV

Biography thus is only at the beginning of its career; it has a long and active life before it, we may be sure--a life full of difficulty, danger, and hard work. Nevertheless, we can also be sure that it is a different life from the life of poetry and fiction--a life lived at a lower degree of tension. And for that reason its creations are not destined for the immortality which the artist now and then achieves for his creations.

There would seem to be certain proof of that already. Even Dr. Johnson as created by Boswell will not live as long as Falstaff as created by Shakespeare. Micawber and Miss Bates we may be certain will survive Lockhart's Sir Walter Scott and Lytton Strachey's Queen Victoria. For they are made of more enduring matter. The artist's imagination at its most intense fires out what is perishable in fact; he builds with what is durable; but the biographer must accept the perishable, build with it, imbed it in the very fabric of his work. Much will perish; little will live. And thus we come to the conclusion, that he is a craftsman, not an artist; and his work is not a work of art, but something betwixt and between.

Yet on that lower level the work of the biographer is invaluable; we cannot thank him sufficiently for what he for us. For we are incapable of living wholly in the intense world of the imagination. The imagination is a faculty that soon tires and needs rest and refreshment. But for a tired imagination the proper food is not inferior poetry or minor fiction--indeed they blunt and debauch it--but sober fact, that "authentic information" from which, as Lytton Strachey has shown us, good biography is made. When and where did the real man live; how did he look; did he wear laced boots or elastic-sided; who were his aunts, and his friends; how did he blow his nose whom did he love, and how; and when he came to die did he die in his bed like a Christian, or . . .

By telling us the true facts, by sifting the little from the big, and shaping the whole so that we perceive the outline, the biographer does more to stimulate the imagination than any poet or novelist save the very greatest. For few poets and novelists are capable of that high degree of tension which gives us reality. But almost any biographer, if he respects facts, can give us much more than another fact to add to our collection. He can give us the creative fact; the fertile fact; the fact that suggests and engenders. Of this, too, there is certain proof. For how often, when a biography is read and tossed aside, some scene remains bright, some figure lives on in the depths of the mind, and causes us, when we read a poem or a novel, to feel a start of recognition, as if we remembered something that we had known before.

CRAFTSMANSHIP
(* A broadcast on April 20th, 1937)

The title of this series is "Words Fail Me," and this particular talk is called "Craftsmanship." We must suppose, therefore, that the talker is meant to discuss the craft of words--the craftsmanship of the writer. But there is something incongruous, unfitting, about the term "craftsmanship" when applied to words. The English dictionary, to which we always turn in moments of dilemma, confirms us in our doubts. It says that the word "craft" has two meanings; it means in the first place making useful objects out of solid matter--for example, a pot, a chair, a table. In the second place, the word "craft" means cajolery, cunning, deceit. Now we know little that is certain about words, but this we do know--words never make anything that is useful; and words are the only things that tell the truth and nothing but the truth. Therefore, to talk of craft in connection with words is to bring together two incongruous ideas, which if they mate can only give birth to some monster fit for a glass case in a museum. Instantly, therefore, the title of the talk must be changed, and for it substituted another--A Ramble round Words, perhaps. For when you cut off the head of a talk it behaves like a hen that has been decapitated. It runs round in a circle till it drops dead--so people say who have killed hens. And that must be the course, or circle, of this decapitated talk. Let us then take for our starting point the statement that words are not useful. This happily needs little proving, for we are all aware of it. When we travel on the Tube, for example, when we wait on the platform for a train, there, hung up in front of us, on an illuminated signboard, are the words "Passing Russell Square." We look at those words; we repeat them; we try to impress that useful fact upon our minds; the next train will pass Russell Square. We say over and over again as we pace, "Passing Russell Square, passing Russell Square." And then as we say them, the words shuffle and change, and we find ourselves saying, "Passing away saith the world, passing away. . . . The leaves decay and fall, the vapours weep their burthen to the ground. Man comes. . . ." And then we wake up and find ourselves at King's Cross.

Take another example. Written up opposite us in the railway carriage are the words: "Do not lean out of the window." At the first reading the useful meaning, the surface meaning, is conveyed; but soon, as we sit looking at the words, they shuffle, they change; and we begin saying, "Windows, yes windows--casements opening on the foam of perilous seas in faery lands forlorn." And before we know what we are doing, we have leant out of the window; we are looking for Ruth in tears amid the alien corn. The penalty for that is twenty pounds or a broken neck.

This proves, if it needs proving, how very little natural gift words have for being useful. If we insist on forcing them against their nature to be useful, we see to our cost how they mislead us, how they fool us, how they land us a crack on the head. We have been so often fooled in this way by words, they have so often proved that they hate being useful, that it is their nature not to express one simple statement but a thousand possibilities--they have done this so often that at last, happily, we are beginning to face the fact. We are beginning to invent another language --a language perfectly and beautifully adapted to express useful statements, a language of signs. There is one great living master of this language to whom we are all indebted, that anonymous writer--whether man, woman or disembodied spirit nobody knows--who describes hotels in the Michelin Guide. He wants to tell us that one hotel is moderate, another good, and a third the best in the place. How does he do it? Not with words; words would at once bring into being shrubberies and billiard tables, men and women, the moon rising and the long splash of the summer sea--all good things, but all here beside the point. He sticks to signs; one gable; two gables; three gables. That is all he says and all he needs to say. Baedeker carries the sign language still further into the sublime realms of art. When he wishes to say that a picture is good, he uses one star; if very good, two stars; when, in his opinion, it is a work of transcendent genius, three black stars shine on the page, and that is all. So with a handful of stars and daggers the whole of art criticism, the whole of literary criticism could be reduced to the size of a sixpenny bit-- there are moments when one could wish it. But this suggests that in time to come writers will have two languages at their service; one for fact, one for fiction. When the biographer has to convey a useful and necessary fact, as, for example, that Oliver Smith went to college and took a third in the year

1892, he will say so with a hollow 0 on top of the figure five. When the novelist is forced to inform us that John rang the bell after a pause the door was opened by a parlourmaid who said, "Mrs. Jones is not at home," he will to our great gain and his own comfort convey that repulsive statement not in words, but in signs--say, a capital H on top of the figure three. Thus we may look forward to the day when our biographies and novels will be slim and muscular; and a railway company that says: "Do not lean out of the window" in words will be fined a penalty not exceeding five pounds for the improper use of language.

Words, then, are not useful. Let us now enquire into their other quality, their positive quality, that is, their power to tell the truth. According once more to the dictionary there are at least three kinds of truth God's or gospel truth; literary truth; and home truth (generally. unflattering). But to consider each separately would take too long. Let us then simplify and assert that since the only test of truth is length of life, and since words survive the chops and changes of time longer than any other substance, therefore they are the truest. Buildings fall; even the earth perishes. What was yesterday a cornfield is to-day a bungalow. But words, if properly used, seem able to live for ever. What, then, we may ask next, is the proper use of words? Not, so we have said, to make a useful statement; for a useful statement is a statement that can mean only one thing. And it is the nature of words to mean many things. Take the simple sentence "Passing Russell Square." That proved useless because besides the surface meaning it contained so many sunken meanings. The word "passing" suggested the transiency of things, the passing of time and the changes of human life. Then the word "Russell" suggested the rustling of leaves and the skirt on a polished floor also the ducal house of Bedford and half the history of England. Finally the word "Square" brings in the sight, the shape of an actual square combined with some visual suggestion of the stark angularity of stucco. Thus one sentence of the simplest kind rouses the imagination, the memory, the eye and the ear--all combine in reading it.

But they combine--they combine unconsciously together. The moment we single out and emphasize the suggestions as we have done here they become unreal; and we, too, become unreal--specialists, word mongers, phrase finders, not readers. In reading we have to allow the sunken meanings to remain sunken, suggested, not stated; lapsing and flowing into each other like reeds on the bed of a river. But the words in that sentence Passing Russell Square-are of course very rudimentary words. They show no trace of the strange, of the diabolical power which words possess when they are not tapped out by a typewriter but come fresh from a human brain--the power that is to suggest the writer; his character, his appearance, his wife, his family, his house--even the cat on the hearthrug. Why words do this, how they do it, how to prevent them from doing it nobody knows. They do it without the writer's will; often against his will. No writer presumably wishes to impose his own miserable character, his own private secrets and vices upon the reader. But has any writer, who is not a typewriter, succeeded in being wholly impersonal? Always, inevitably, we know them as well as their books. Such is the suggestive power of words that they will often make a bad book into a very lovable human being, and a good book into a man whom we can hardly tolerate in the room. Even words that are hundreds of years old have this power; when they are new they have it so strongly that they deafen us to the writer's meaning--it is them we see, them we hear. That is one reason why our judgments of living writers are so wildly erratic. Only after the writer is dead do his words to some extent become disinfected, purified of the accidents of the living body.

Now, this power of suggestion is one of the most mysterious properties of words. Everyone who has ever written a sentence must be conscious or half-conscious of it. Words, English words, are full of echoes, of memories, of associations--naturally. They have been out and about, on people's lips, in their houses, in the streets, in the fields, for so many centuries. And that is one of the chief difficulties in writing them today--that they are so stored with meanings, with memories, that they have contracted so many famous marriages. The splendid word "incarnadine," for example--who can use it without remembering also "multitudinous seas"? In the old days, of course, when English was a new language, writers could invent new words and use them. Nowadays it is easy enough to invent new words--they spring to the lips whenever we see a new sight or feel a new sensation--but we cannot use them because the language is old. You cannot use a brand new word in an old language because of the very obvious yet mysterious fact that a word is not a single and separate entity, but part of other words. It is not a word indeed until it is part of a sentence. Words belong to each other, although, of course, only a great writer knows that the word "incarnadine" belongs to "multitudinous seas." To combine new words with old words is fatal to the constitution of the sentence. In order to use new words properly you would have to invent a new language; and that, though no doubt we shall come to it, is not at the moment our business. Our business is to see what we can do with the English language as it is. How can we combine the old words in new orders so that they survive, so that they create beauty, so that they tell the truth? That is the question.

And the person who could answer that question would deserve whatever crown of glory the world has to offer. Think what it would mean if you could teach, if you could learn, the art of writing. Why, every book, every newspaper would tell the truth, would create beauty. But there is, it would appear, some obstacle in the way, some hindrance to the teaching of words. For though at this moment at least a hundred professors are lecturing upon the literature of the past, at least a thousand critics are reviewing the literature of the present, and hundreds upon hundreds of young men and women are passing examinations in English literature with the utmost credit, still--do we write better, do we read better than we read and wrote four hundred years ago when we were unlectured, uncriticized, untaught? Is our

Georgian literature a patch on the Elizabethan? Where then are we to lay the blame? Not on our professors; not on our reviewers; not on our writers; but on words. It is words that are to blame. They are the wildest, freest, most irresponsible, most unteachable of all things. Of course, you can catch them and sort them and place them in alphabetical order in dictionaries. But words do not live in dictionaries; they live in the mind. If you want proof of this, consider how often in moments of emotion when we most need words we find none. Yet there is the dictionary; there at our disposal are some half-a-million words all in alphabetical order. But can we use them? No, because words do not live in dictionaries, they live in the mind. Look again at the dictionary. There beyond a doubt lie plays more splendid than ANTONY AND CLEOPATRA; poems more lovely than the ODE TO A NIGHTINGALE; novels beside which PRIDE AND PREJUDICE or DAVID COPPERFIELD are the crude bunglings of amateurs. It is only a question of finding the right words and putting them in the right order. But we cannot do it because they do not live in dictionaries; they live in the mind. And how do they live in the mind? Variously and strangely, much as human beings live, by ranging hither and thither, by falling in love, and mating together. It is true that they are much less bound by ceremony and convention than we are. Royal words mate with commoners. English words marry French words, German words, Indian words, Negro words, if they have a fancy. Indeed, the less we enquire into the past of our dear Mother English the better it will be for that lady's reputation. For she has gone a-roving, a-roving fair maid.

Thus to lay down any laws for such irreclaimable vagabonds is worse than useless. A few trifling rules of grammar and spelling are all the constraint we can put on them. All we can say about them, as we peer at them over the edge of that deep, dark and only fitfully illuminated cavern in which they live--the mind--all we can say about them is that they seem to like people to think and to feel before they use them, but to think and to feel not about them, but about something different. They are highly sensitive, easily made self-conscious. They do not like to have their purity or their impurity discussed. If you start a Society for Pure English, they will show their resentment by starting another for impure English--hence the unnatural violence of much modern speech; it is a protest against the puritans. They are highly democratic, too; they believe that one word is as good as another; uneducated words are as good as educated words, uncultivated words as cultivated words, there are no ranks or titles in their society. Nor do they like being lifted out on the point of a pen and examined separately. They hang together, in sentences, in paragraphs, sometimes for whole pages at a time. They hate being useful; they hate making money; they hate being lectured about in public. In short, they hate anything that stamps them with one meaning or confines them to one attitude, for it is their nature to change.

Perhaps that is their most striking peculiarity--their need of change. It is because the truth they try to catch is many-sided, and they convey it by being themselves many-sided, flashing this way, then that. Thus they mean one thing to one person, another thing to another person; they are unintelligible to one generation, plain as a pikestaff to the next. And it is because of this complexity that they survive. Perhaps then one reason why we have no great poet, novelist or critic writing to-day is that we refuse words their liberty. We pin them down to one meaning, their useful meaning, the meaning which makes us catch the train, the meaning which makes us pass the examination. And when words are pinned down they fold their wings and die. Finally, and most emphatically, words, like ourselves, in order to live at their ease, need privacy. Undoubtedly they like us to think, and they like us to feel, before we use them; but they also like us to pause; to become unconscious. Our unconsciousness is their privacy; our darkness is their light. . . . That pause was made, that veil of darkness was dropped, to tempt words to come together in one of those swift marriages which are perfect images and create everlasting beauty. But no--nothing of that sort is going to happen to-night. The little wretches are out of temper; disobliging; disobedient; dumb. What is it that they are muttering? "Time's up! Silence!"

A LETTER TO A YOUNG POET
(* Written in 1932.)

My Dear John,

Did you ever meet, or was he before your day, that old gentleman--I forget his name--who used to enliven conversation, especially at breakfast when the post came in, by saying that the art of letter-writing is dead? The penny post, the old gentleman used to say, has killed the art of letter-writing. Nobody, he continued, examining an envelope through his eye-glasses, has the time even to cross their t's. We rush, he went on, spreading his toast with marmalade, to the telephone. We commit our half-formed thoughts in ungrammatical phrases to the post card. Gray is dead, he continued; Horace Walpole is dead; Madame de Sévigné--she is dead too, I suppose he was about to add, but a fit of choking cut him short, and he had to leave the room before he had time to condemn all the arts, as his pleasure was, to the cemetery. But when the post came in this morning and I opened your letter stuffed with little blue sheets written all over in a cramped but not illegible hand--I regret to say, however, that several t's were uncrossed and the grammar of one sentence seems to me dubious--I replied after all these years to that elderly necrophilist--Nonsense. The art of letter-writing has only just come into existence. It is the child of the penny post. And there is some truth in that remark, I think. Naturally when a letter cost half a crown to send, it had to prove itself a document of some importance; it was read aloud; it was tied up with green silk; after a certain number of years it was published for the infinite delectation of posterity. But your letter, on the contrary, will have to be burnt. It only cost three-halfpence to send. Therefore you could afford to be intimate, irreticent, indiscreet in the extreme. What you tell me about poor dear C. and his adventure on the Channel boat is deadly private; your ribald jests at the expense of M. would certainly ruin your friendship if they got about; I doubt, too, that posterity, unless it is much quicker in the wit than I expect, could follow the line of your thought from the roof which leaks ("splash, splash, splash into the soap dish") past Mrs. Gape, the charwoman, whose retort to the greengrocer gives me the keenest pleasure, via Miss Curtis and her odd confidence on the steps of the omnibus; to Siamese cats ("Wrap their noses in an old stocking my Aunt says if they howl"); so to the value of criticism to a writer; so to Donne; so to Gerard Hopkins; so to tombstones; so to gold-fish; and so with a sudden alarming swoop to "Do write and tell me where poetry's going, or if it's dead?" No, your letter, because it is a true letter--one that can neither be read aloud now, nor printed in time to come--will have to be burnt. Posterity must live upon Walpole and Madame de Sévigné. The great age of letter-writing, which is, of course, the present, will leave no letters behind it. And in making my reply there is only one question that I can answer or attempt to answer in public; about poetry and its death.

But before I begin, I must own up to those defects, both natural and acquired, which, as you will find, distort and invalidate all that I have to say about poetry. The lack of a sound university training has always made it impossible for me to distinguish between an iambic and a dactyl, and if this were not enough to condemn one for ever, the practice of prose has bred in me, as in most prose writers, a foolish jealousy, a righteous indignation--anyhow, an emotion which the critic should be without. For how, we despised prose writers ask when we get together, could one say what one meant and observe the rules of poetry? Conceive dragging in "blade" because one had mentioned "maid"; and pairing "sorrow" with "borrow"? Rhyme is not only childish, but dishonest, we prose writers say. Then we go on to say, And look at their rules! How easy to be a poet! How strait the path is for them, and how strict! This you must do; this you must not. I would rather be a child and walk in a crocodile down a suburban path than write poetry, I have heard prose writers say. It must be like taking the veil and entering a religious order--observing the rites and rigours of metre. That explains why they repeat the same thing over and over again. Whereas we prose writers (I am only telling you the sort of nonsense prose writers talk when they are alone) are masters of language, not its slaves; nobody can teach us; nobody can coerce us; we say what we mean; we have the whole of life for our province. We are the creators, we are the explorers.... So we run on--nonsensically enough, I must admit.

Now that I have made a clean breast of these deficiencies, let us proceed. From certain phrases in your letter I gather that you think that poetry is in a parlous way, and that your case as a poet in this particular autumn Of 1931 is a great deal harder than Shakespeare's, Dryden's, Pope's, or Tennyson's. In fact it is the hardest case that has ever been known. Here you give me an opening, which I am prompt to seize, for a little lecture. Never think yourself singular, never think your own case much harder than other people's. I admit that the age we live in makes this difficult. For the first time in history there are readers--a large body of people, occupied in business, in sport, in nursing their grandfathers, in tying up parcels behind counters--they all read now; and they want to be told how to read and what to read; and their teachers--the reviewers, the lecturers, the broadcasters--must in all humanity make reading easy for them; assure them that literature is violent and exciting, full of heroes and villains; of hostile forces perpetually in conflict; of fields strewn with bones; of solitary victors riding off on white horses wrapped in black cloaks to meet their death at the turn of the road. A pistol shot rings out. "The age of romance was over. The age of realism had begun"--you know the sort of thing. Now of course writers themselves know very well that there is not a word of truth in all this--there are no battles, and no murders and no defeats and no victories. But as it is of the utmost importance that readers should be amused, writers acquiesce. They dress themselves up. They act their parts. One leads; the other follows. One is romantic, the other realist. One is advanced, the other out of date. There is no harm in it, so long as you take it as a joke, but once you believe in it, once you begin to take yourself seriously as a leader or as a follower, as a modern or as a conservative, then you become a self-conscious, biting, and scratching little animal whose work is not of the slightest value or importance to anybody. Think of yourself rather as something much humbler and less spectacular, but to my mind, far more interesting--a poet in whom live all the poets of the past, from whom all poets in time to come will spring. You have a touch of Chaucer in you, and something of Shakespeare; Dryden, Pope, Tennyson-- to mention only the respectable among your ancestors--stir in your blood and sometimes move your pen a little to the right or to the left. In short you are an immensely ancient, complex, and continuous character, for which reason please treat yourself with respect and think twice before you dress up as Guy Fawkes and spring out upon timid old ladies at street corners, threatening death and demanding twopence-halfpenny.

However, as you say that you are in a fix ("it has never been so hard to write poetry as it is to-day and that poetry may be, you think, at its last gasp in England the novelists are doing all the interesting things now"), let me while away the time before the post goes in imagining your state and in hazarding one or two guesses which, since this is a letter, need not be taken too seriously or pressed too far. Let me try to put myself in your place; let me try to imagine, with your letter to help me, what it feels like to be a young poet in the autumn of 1931. (And taking my own advice, I shall treat you not as one poet in particular, but as several poets in one.) On the floor of your mind, then--is it not this that makes you a poet?--rhythm keeps up its perpetual beat. Sometimes it seems to die down to nothing; it lets you eat, sleep, talk like other people. Then again it swells and rises and attempts to sweep all the contents of your mind into one dominant dance. To-night is such an occasion. Although you are alone, and have taken one boot off and are about to undo the other, you cannot go on with the process of undressing, but must instantly write at the bidding of the dance. You snatch pen and paper; you hardly trouble to hold the one or to straighten the other. And while you write, while the first stanzas of the dance are being fastened down, I will withdraw a little and look out of the window. A woman passes, then a man; a car glides to a stop and then--but there is no need to say what I see out of the window, nor indeed is there time, for I am suddenly recalled from my observations by a cry of rage or despair. Your page is crumpled in a ball; your pen sticks upright by the nib in the carpet. If there were a cat to swing or a wife to murder now would be the time. So at least I infer from the ferocity of your expression. You are rasped, jarred, thoroughly out of temper. And if I am to guess the reason, it is, I should say, that the rhythm which was opening and shutting with a force that sent shocks of excitement from your head to your heels has encountered some hard and hostile object upon which it has smashed itself to pieces. Something has worked in which cannot be made into poetry; some foreign body, angular, sharp-edged, gritty, has refused to join in the dance. Obviously, suspicion attaches to Mrs. Gape; she has asked you to make a poem of her; then to

Miss Curtis and her confidences on the omnibus; then to C., who has infected you with a wish to tell his story--and a very amusing one it was--in verse. But for some reason you cannot do their bidding. Chaucer could; Shakespeare could; so could Crabbe, Byron, and perhaps Robert Browning. But it is October 1931, and for a long time now poetry has shirked contact with--what shall we call it?--Shall we shortly and no doubt inaccurately call it life? And will you come to my help by guessing what I mean? Well then, it has left all that to the novelist. Here you see how easy it would be for me to write two or three volumes in honour of prose and in mockery of verse; to say how wide and ample is the domain of the one, how starved and stunted the little grove of the other. But it would be simpler and perhaps fairer to check these theories by opening one of the thin books of modern verse that lie on your table. I open and I find myself instantly confused. Here are the common objects of daily prose--the bicycle and the omnibus. Obviously the poet is making his muse face facts. Listen:

Which of you waking early and watching daybreak Will not hasten in heart, handsome, aware of wonder At light unleashed, advancing; a leader of movement, Breaking like surf on turf on road and roof, Or chasing shadow on downs like whippet racing, The stilled stone, halting at eyelash barrier, Enforcing in face a profile, marks of misuse, Beating impatient and importunate on boudoir shutters Where the old life is not up yet, with rays Exploring through rotting floor a dismantled mill-- The old life never to be born again?

Yes, but how will he get through with it? I read on and find:

Whistling as he shuts His door behind him, travelling to work by tube Or walking to the park to it to ease the bowels,

and read on and find again

As a boy lately come up from country to town Returns for the day to his village in EXPENSIVE SHOES--

and so on again to:

Seeking a heaven on earth he chases his shadow, Loses his capital and his nerve in pursuing What yachtsmen, explorers, climbers and BUGGERS ARE AFTER.

These lines and the words I have emphasized are enough to confirm me in part of my guess at least. The poet is trying to include Mrs. Gape. He is honestly of opinion that she can be brought into poetry and will do very well there. Poetry, he feels, will be improved by the actual, the colloquial. But though I honour him for the attempt, I doubt that it is wholly successful. I feel a jar. I feel a shock. I feel as if I had stubbed my toe on the corner of the wardrobe. Am I then, I go on to ask, shocked, prudishly and conventionally, by the words themselves? I think not. The shock is literally a shock. The poet as I guess has strained himself to include an emotion that is not domesticated and acclimatized to poetry; the effort has thrown him off his balance; he rights himself, as I am sure I shall find if I turn the page, by a violent recourse to the poetical--he invokes the moon or the nightingale. Anyhow, the transition is sharp. The poem is cracked in the middle. Look, it comes apart in my hands: here is reality on one side, here is beauty on the other; and instead of acquiring a whole object rounded and entire, I am left with broken parts in my hands which, since my reason has been roused and my imagination has not been allowed to take entire possession of me, I contemplate coldly, critically, and with distaste.

Such at least is the hasty analysis I make of my own sensations as a reader; but again I am interrupted. I see that you have overcome your difficulty, whatever it was; the pen is once more in action, and having torn up the first poem you are at work upon another. Now then if I want to understand your state of mind I must invent another explanation to account for this return of fluency. You have dismissed, as I suppose, all sorts of things that would come naturally to your pen if you had been writing prose--the charwoman, the omnibus, the incident on the Channel boat. Your range is restricted--I judge from your expression--concentrated and intensified. I hazard a guess that you are thinking now, not about things in general, but about yourself in particular. There is a fixity, a gloom, yet an inner glow that seem to hint that you are looking within and not without. But in order to consolidate these flimsy guesses about the meaning of an expression on a face, let me open another of the books on your table and check it by what I find there. Again I open at random and read this:

To penetrate that room is my desire, The extreme attic of the mind, that lies Just beyond the last bend in the corridor. Writing I do it. Phrases, poems are keys. Loving's another way (but not so sure). A fire's in there, I think, there's truth at last Deep in a lumber chest. Sometimes I'm near, But draughts puff out the matches, and I'm lost. Sometimes I'm lucky, find a key to turn, Open an inch or two--but always then A bell rings, someone calls, or cries of "fire" Arrest my hand when nothing's known or seen, And running down the stairs again I mourn.

and then this:

There is a dark room, The locked and shuttered womb, Where negative's made positive. Another dark room, The blind and bolted tomb, Where positives change to negative. We may not undo that or escape this, who Have birth and death coiled in our bones, Nothing we can do Will sweeten the real rue, That we begin, and end, with groans.

And then this:

Never being, but always at the edge of Being My head, like Death mask, is brought into the Sun. The shadow pointing finger across cheek, I move lips for tasting, I move hands for touching, But never am nearer than touching, Though the spirit leans outward for seeing. Observing rose, gold, eyes, an admired landscape, My senses record the act of wishing Wishing to be Rose, gold, landscape or another-- Claiming fulfilment in the act of loving.

Since these quotations are chosen at random and I have yet found three different poets writing about nothing, if not about the poet himself, I hold that the chances are that you too are engaged in the same occupation. I conclude that self offers no impediment; self joins in the dance; self lends itself to the rhythm; it is apparently easier to write a poem about oneself than about any other subject. But what does one mean by "oneself"? Not the self that Wordsworth, Keats, and Shelley have described--not the self that loves a woman, or that hates a tyrant, or that broods over the mystery of the world. No, the self that you are engaged in describing is shut out from all that. It is a self that sits alone in the room at night with the blinds drawn. In other words the poet is much less interested in what we have in common than in what he has apart. Hence I suppose the extreme difficulty of these poems--and I have to confess that it would floor me completely to say from one reading or even from two or three what these poems mean. The poet is trying honestly and exactly to describe a world that has perhaps no existence except for one particular person at one particular moment. And the more sincere he is in keeping to the precise outline of the roses and cabbages of his private universe, the more he puzzles us who have agreed in a lazy spirit of compromise to see roses and cabbages as they are seen, more or less, by the twenty-six passengers on the outside of an omnibus. He strains to describe; we strain to see; he flickers his torch; we catch a flying gleam. It is exciting; it is stimulating; but is that a tree, we ask, or is it perhaps an old woman tying up her shoe in the gutter?

Well, then, if there is any truth in what I am saying--if that is you cannot write about the actual, the colloquial, Mrs. Gape or the Channel boat or Miss Curtis on the omnibus, without straining the machine of poetry, if, therefore, you are driven to contemplate landscapes and emotions within and must render visible to the world at large what you alone can see, then indeed yours is a hard case, and poetry, though still breathing--witness these little books--is drawing her breath in short, sharp gasps. Still, consider the symptoms. They are not the symptoms of death in the least. Death in literature, and I need not tell you how often literature has died in this country or in that, comes gracefully, smoothly, quietly. Lines slip easily down the accustomed grooves. The old designs are copied so glibly that we are half inclined to think them original, save for that very glibness. But here the very opposite is happening: here in my first quotation the poet breaks his machine because he will clog it with raw fact. In my second, he is unintelligible because of his desperate determination to tell the truth about himself. Thus I cannot help thinking that though you may be right in talking of the difficulty of the time, you are wrong to despair.

Is there not, alas, good reason to hope? I say "alas" because then I must give my reasons, which are bound to be foolish and certain also to cause pain to the large and highly respectable society of necrophils--Mr. Peabody, and his like-- who much prefer death to life and are even now intoning the sacred and comfortable words, Keats is dead, Shelley is dead, Byron is dead. But it is late: necrophily induces slumber; the old gentlemen have fallen asleep over their classics, and if what I am about to say takes a sanguine tone--and for my part I do not believe in poets dying; Keats, Shelley, Byron are alive here in this room in you and you and you--I can take comfort from the thought that my hoping will not disturb their snoring. So to continue--why should not poetry, now that it has so honestly scraped itself free from certain falsities, the wreckage of the great Victorian age, now that it has so sincerely gone down into the mind of the poet and verified its outlines--a work of renovation that has to be done from time to time and was certainly needed, for bad poetry is almost always the result of forgetting oneself--all becomes distorted and impure if you lose sight of that central reality--now, I say, that poetry has done all this, why should it not once more open its eyes, look out of the window and write about other people? Two or three hundred years ago you were always writing about other people. Your pages were crammed with characters of the most opposite and various kinds--Hamlet, Cleopatra, Falstaff. Not only did we go to you for drama, and for the subtleties of human character, but we also went to you, incredible though this now seems, for laughter. You made us roar with laughter. Then later, not more than a hundred years ago, you were lashing our follies, trouncing our hypocrisies, and dashing off the most brilliant of satires. You were Byron, remember; you wrote Don Juan. You were Crabbe also; you took the most sordid details of the lives of peasants for your theme. Clearly therefore you have it in you to deal with a vast variety of subjects; it is only a temporary necessity that has shut you up in one room, alone, by yourself.

But how are you going to get out, into the world of other people? That is your problem now, if I may hazard a guess--to find the right relationship, now that you know yourself, between the self that you know and the world outside. It is a difficult problem. No living poet has, I think, altogether solved it. And there are a thousand voices prophesying despair. Science, they say, has made poetry impossible; there is no poetry in motor cars and wireless. And we have no religion. All is tumultuous and transitional. Therefore, so people say, there can be no relation between the poet and the present age. But surely that is nonsense. These accidents are superficial; they do not go nearly deep enough to destroy the most profound and primitive of instincts, the instinct of rhythm. All you need now is to stand at the window and let your rhythmical sense open and shut, open and shut, boldly and freely, until one thing melts in another, until the taxis are dancing with the daffodils, until a whole has been made from all these separate fragments. I am talking nonsense, I know. What I mean is, summon all your courage, exert all your vigilance, invoke all the gifts that Nature has been induced to bestow. Then let your rhythmical sense wind itself in and out among men and women, omnibuses, sparrows--whatever come along the street--until it has strung them together in one harmonious whole. That perhaps is your task--to find the relation between things that seem incompatible yet have a mysterious affinity, to absorb every experience that comes your way fearlessly and saturate it completely so that your poem is a whole, not a fragment; to re-think human life into poetry and so give us tragedy again and comedy by means of characters not spun out at length in the novelist's way, but condensed and synthesised in the poet's way-that is what we look to you to do now. But as I do not know what I mean by rhythm nor what I mean by life, and as most certainly I cannot tell you which objects can properly be combined together in a poem--that is entirely your affair--and as I cannot tell a dactyl from an iambic, and am therefore unable to say how you must modify and expand the rites and ceremonies of your ancient and mysterious art--I will move on to safer ground and turn again to these little books themselves.

When, then, I return to them I am, as I have admitted, filled, not with forebodings of death, but with hopes for the future. But one does not always want to be thinking of the future, if, as sometimes happens, one is living in the present. When I read these poems, now, at the present moment, I find myself--reading, you know, is rather like opening the door to a horde of rebels who swarm out attacking one in twenty places at once--hit, roused, scraped, bared, swung through the air, so that life seems to flash by; then again blinded, knocked on the head--all of which are agreeable sensations for a reader (since nothing is more dismal than to open the door and get no response), and all I believe certain proof that this poet is alive and kicking. And yet mingling with these cries of delight, of jubilation, I record also, as I read, the repetition in the bass of one word intoned over and over again by some malcontent. At last then, silencing the others, I say to this malcontent, "Well, and what do YOU want?" Whereupon he bursts out, rather to my discomfort, "Beauty." Let me repeat, I take no responsibility for what my senses say when I read; I merely record the fact that there is a malcontent in me who complains that it seems to him odd, considering that English is a mixed language, a rich language; a language unmatched for its sound and colour, for its power of imagery and suggestion--it seems to him odd that these modern poets should write as if they had neither ears nor eyes, neither soles to their feet nor palms to their hands, but only honest enterprising book-fed brains, uni-sexual bodies and--but here I interrupted him. For when it comes to saying that a poet should be bisexual, and that I think is what he was about to say, even I, who have had no scientific training whatsoever, draw the line and tell that voice to be silent.

But how far, if we discount these obvious absurdities, do you think there is truth in this complaint? For my own part now that I have stopped reading, and can see the poems more or less as a whole, I think it is true that the eye and ear are starved of their rights. There is no sense of riches held in reserve behind the admirable exactitude of the lines I have quoted, as there is, for example, behind the exactitude of Mr. Yeats. The poet clings to his one word, his only word, as a drowning man to a spar. And if this is so, I am ready to hazard a reason for it all the more readily because I think it bears out what I have just been saying. The art of writing, and that is perhaps what my malcontent means by "beauty," the art of having at one's beck and call every word in the language, of knowing their weights, colours, sounds, associations, and thus making them, as is so necessary in English, suggest more than they can state, can be learnt of course to some extent by reading--it is impossible to read too much; but much more drastically and effectively by imagining that one is not oneself but somebody different. How can you learn to write if you write only about one single person? To take the obvious example. Can you doubt that the reason why Shakespeare knew every sound and syllable in the language and could do precisely what he liked with grammar and syntax, was that Hamlet, Falstaff and Cleopatra rushed him into this knowledge; that the lords, officers, dependants, murderers and common soldiers of the plays insisted that he should say exactly what they felt in the words expressing their feelings? It was they who taught him to write, not the begetter of the Sonnets. So that if you want to satisfy all those senses that rise in a swarm whenever we drop a poem among them--the reason, the imagination, the eyes, the ears, the palms of the hands and the soles of the feet, not to mention a million more that the psychologists have yet to name, you will do well to embark upon a long poem in which people as unlike yourself as possible talk at the tops of their voices. And for heaven's sake, publish nothing before you are thirty.

That, I am sure, is of very great importance. Most of the faults in the poems I have been reading can be explained, I think, by the fact that they have been exposed to the fierce light of publicity while they were still too young to stand the strain. It has shrivelled them into a skeleton austerity, both emotional and verbal, which should not be characteristic of youth. The poet writes very well; he writes for the eye of a severe and intelligent public; but how much better he would have written if for ten years he had written for no eye but his own! After all, the years from twenty to thirty are years (let me refer to your letter again) of emotional excitement. The rain dripping, a wing flashing, someone passing--the commonest sounds and sights have power to fling one, as I seem to remember, from the heights of rapture to the depths of despair. And if the actual life is thus extreme, the visionary life should be free to follow. Write then, now that you are young, nonsense by the ream. Be silly, be sentimental, imitate Shelley, imitate Samuel Smiles; give the rein to every impulse; commit every fault of style, grammar, taste, and syntax; pour out; tumble over; loose anger, love, satire, in whatever words you can catch, coerce or create, in whatever metre, prose, poetry, or gibberish that comes to hand. Thus you will learn to write. But if you publish, your freedom will be checked; you will be thinking what people will say; you will write for others when you ought only to be writing for yourself. And what point can there be in curbing the wild torrent of spontaneous nonsense which is now, for a few years only, your divine gift in order to publish prim little books of experimental verses? To make money? That, we both know, is out of the question. To get criticism? But you friends will pepper your manuscripts with far more serious and searching criticism than any you will get from the reviewers. As for fame, look I implore you at famous people; see how the waters of dullness spread around them as they enter; observe their pomposity, their prophetic airs; reflect that the greatest poets were anonymous; think how Shakespeare cared nothing for fame; how Donne tossed his poems into the waste-paper basket;

write an essay giving a single instance of any modern English writer who has survived the disciples and the admirers, the autograph hunters and the interviewers, the dinners and the luncheons, the celebrations and the commemorations with which English society so effectively stops the mouths of its singers and silences their songs.

But enough. I, at any rate, refuse to be necrophilus. So long as you and you and you, venerable and ancient representatives of Sappho, Shakespeare, and Shelley are aged precisely twenty-three and propose--0 enviable lot!-- to spend the next fifty years of your lives in writing poetry, I refuse to think that the art is dead. And if ever the temptation to necrophilize comes over you, be warned by the fate of that old gentleman whose name I forget, but I think that it was Peabody. In the very act of consigning all the arts to the grave he choked over a large piece of hot buttered toast and the consolation then offered him that he was about to join the elder Pliny in the shades gave him, I am told, no sort of satisfaction whatsoever.

And now for the intimate, the indiscreet, and indeed, the only really interesting parts of this letter. . . .

WHY?

When the first number of LYSISTRATA appeared, I confess that I was deeply disappointed. It was so well printed, on such good paper. It looked established, prosperous. As I turned the pages it seemed to me that wealth must have descended upon Somerville, and I was about to answer the request of the editor for an article with a negative, when I read, greatly to my relief, that one of the writers was badly dressed, and gathered from another that the women's colleges still lack power and prestige. At this I plucked up heart, and a crowd of questions that have been pressing to be asked rushed to my lips saying: "Here is our chance."

I should explain that like so many people nowadays I am pestered with questions. I find it impossible to walk down the street without stopping, it may be in the middle of the road. to ask: Why? Churches, public houses, parliaments, shops, loud speakers, motor cars, the drone of an aeroplane in the clouds, and men and women all inspire questions. Yet what is the point of asking questions of oneself? They should be asked openly in public. But the great obstacle to asking questions openly in public is, of course, wealth. The little twisted sign that comes at the end of a question has a way of making the rich writhe; power and prestige come down upon it with all their weight. Questions, therefore, being sensitive, impulsive and often foolish, have a way of picking their asking place with care. They shrivel up in an atmosphere of power, prosperity, and time-worn stone. They die by the dozen on the threshold of great newspaper offices. They slink away to less favoured, less flourishing quarters where people are poor and therefore have nothing to give, where they have no power and therefore have nothing to lose. Now the questions that have been pestering me to ask them decided, whether rightly or wrongly, that they could be asked in LYSISTRATA. They said: "We do not expect you to ask us in----," here they named some of our most respectable dailies and weeklies; "nor in----," here they named some of our most venerable institutions. "But, thank Heaven!" they exclaimed, "are not women's colleges poor and young? Are they not inventive, adventurous? Are they not out to create a new----"

"The editor forbids feminism," I interposed severely.

"What is feminism?" they screamed with one accord, and as I did not answer at once, a new question was flung at me: "Don't you think it high time that a new----"

But I stopped them by reminding them that they had only two thousand words at their disposal. Upon that, they withdrew, consulted together, and finally put forward the request that I should introduce one or two of them of the simplest, tamest, and most obvious. For example, there is the question that always bobs up at the beginning of term when societies issue their invitations and universities open their doors--why lecture, why be lectured?

In order to place this question fairly before you, I will describe, for memory has kept the picture bright, one of those rare but, as Queen Victoria would have put at, never-to-be-sufficiently-lamented occasions when in deference to friendship, or in a desperate attempt to acquire information about, perhaps, the French Revolution, it seemed necessary to attend a lecture. The room to begin with had a hybrid look--it was not for sitting in, nor yet for eating in. Perhaps there was a map on the wall; certainly there was a table on a platform, and several rows of rather small, rather hard, comfortless little chairs. These were occupied intermittently, as if they shunned each other's company, by people of both sexes, and some had notebooks and were tapping their fountain pens, and some had none and gazed with the vacancy and placidity of bull frogs at the ceiling. A large clock displayed its cheerless face,--and when the hour struck in strode a harried-looking man, a man from whose face nervousness, vanity, or perhaps the depressing and impossible nature of his task had removed all traces of ordinary humanity. There was a momentary stir. He had written a book, and for a moment it is interesting to see people who have written books. Everybody gazed at him. He was bald and not hairy; had a mouth and a chin; in short he was a man like another, although he had written a book. He cleared his throat and the lecture began. Now the human voice is an instrument of varied power; it can enchant and it can soothe; it can rage and it can despair; but when it lectures it almost always bores. What he said was sensible enough; there was learning in it and argument and reason; but as the voice went on attention wandered. The face of the clock seemed abnormally pale; the hands too suffered from some infirmity. Had they the gout? Were they swollen? They moved so slowly. They reminded one of the painful progress of a three-legged fly that has survived the winter. How many flies on an average survive the English winter, and what would be the thoughts of such an insect on waking to find itself being lectured on the French Revolution? The enquiry was fatal. A link had been lost--a paragraph dropped. It was useless to ask the lecturer to repeat his words; on he plodded with dogged pertinacity. The origin of the French Revolution was being sought for--also the thoughts of flies. Now there came one of those flat stretches of discourse when minute objects can be seen coming for two or three miles ahead. "Skip!" we entreated him--vainly. He did not skip. There was a joke. Then the voice went on again; then it seemed that the windows wanted washing; then a woman sneezed; then the voice quickened; then there was a peroration and then-- thank Heaven!--the lecture was over.

Why, since life holds only so many hours, waste one of them on being lectured? Why, since printing presses have been invented these many centuries, should he not have printed his lecture instead of speaking it? Then, by the fire in winter, or under an apple tree in summer, it could have been read, thought over, discussed; the difficult ideas pondered, the argument debated. It could have been thickened and stiffened. There would have been no need of those repetitions and dilutions with which lectures have to be watered down and brightened up, so as to attract the attention of a miscellaneous audience too apt to think about noses and chins, women sneezing and the longevity of flies.

It may be, I told these questions, that there is some reason, imperceptible to outsiders, which makes lectures an essential part of university discipline. But why--here another rushed to the forefront--why, if lectures are necessary as a form of education, should they not be abolished as a form of entertainment? Never does the crocus flower or the beech tree redden but there issues simultaneously from all the universities of England, Scotland and Ireland a shower of notes from desperate secretaries entreating So-and-so and So-and-so and So-and-so to come down and address them upon art or literature or politics or morality--And why?

In the old days, when newspapers were scarce and carefully lent about from hall to rectory, such laboured methods of rubbing up minds and imparting ideas were no doubt essential. But now, when every day of the week scatters our tables with articles and pamphlets in which every shade of opinion is expressed, far more tersely than by word of mouth, why continue an obsolete custom which not merely wastes time and temper, but incites the most debased of human passions--vanity, ostentation, self-assertion, and the desire to convert? Why encourage your elders to turn themselves into prigs and prophets, when they are ordinary men and women? Why force them to stand on a platform for forty minutes while you reflect upon the colour of their hair and the longevity of flies? Why not let them talk to you and listen to you, naturally and happily, on the floor? Why not create a new form of society founded on poverty and equality? Why not bring together people of all ages and both sexes and all shades of fame and obscurity so that they can talk, without mounting platforms or reading papers or wearing expensive clothes or eating expensive food? Would not such a society be worth, even as a form of education, all the papers on art and literature that have ever been read since the world began? Why not abolish prigs and prophets? Why not invent human intercourse? Why not try?

Here, being sick of the word "why," I was about to indulge myself with a few reflections of a general nature upon society as it was, as it is, as it might be, with a few fancy pictures of Mrs. Thrale entertaining Dr. Johnson, Lady Holland amusing Lord Macaulay thrown in, when such a clamour arose among the questions that I could hardly hear myself think. The cause of the clamour was soon apparent. I had incautiously and foolishly used the word "literature." Now if there is one word that excites questions and puts them in a fury it is this word "literature." There they were, screaming and crying, asking questions about poetry and fiction and criticism, each demanding to be heard, each certain that his was the only question that deserved an answer. At last, when they had destroyed all my fancy pictures of Lady Holland and Dr. Johnson, one insisted, for he said that foolish and rash as he might be he was less so than the others, that he should be asked. And his question was, why learn English literature at universities when you can read it for yourselves in books? But I said that it is foolish to ask a question that has already been answered--English literature is, I believe, already taught at the universities. Besides, if we are going to start an argument about it, we should need at least twenty volumes, whereas we have only about seven hundred words remaining. Still, as he was importunate, I said I would ask the question and introduce it to the best of my ability, without expressing any opinion of my own, by copying down the following fragment of dialogue.

The other day I went to call upon a friend of mine who earns her living as a publisher's reader. The room was a little dark, it seemed to me, when I went in. Yet, as the window was open and it was a fine spring day, the darkness must have been spiritual--the effect of some private sorrow I feared. Her first words as I came in confirmed my fears:

"Alas, poor boy!" she exclaimed, tossing the manuscript she was reading to the ground with a gesture of despair. Had some accident happened to one of her relations, I asked, motoring or climbing?

"If you call three hundred pages on the evolution of the Elizabethan sonnet an accident." she said.

"Is that all?" I replied with relief.

"All?" she retaliated, "Isn't it enough?" And, beginning to pace up and down the room she exclaimed: "Once he was a clever boy; once he was worth talking to; once he cared about English literature. But now----" She threw out her hands as if words failed her--but not at all. There followed such a flood of lamentation and vituperation--but reflecting how hard her life was, reading manuscripts day in, day out, I excused her--that I could not follow the argument. All I could gather was that this lecturing about English literature-

-"if you want to teach them to read English," she threw in, "teach them to read Greek"--this passing of examinations in English literature, which led to all this writing about English literature, was bound in the end to be the death and burial of English literature. "The tombstone," she was proceeding, "will be a bound volume of----" when I stopped her and told her not to talk such nonsense. "Then tell me," she said, standing over me with her fists clenched, "do they write any better for it? Is poetry better, is fiction better, is criticism better now that they have been taught how to read English literature?" As if to answer her own question she read a passage from the manuscript on the floor. "And each the spit and image of the other!" she groaned, lifting it wearily to its place with the manuscripts on the shelf.

"But think of all they must know," I tried to argue.

"Know?" she echoed me. "Know? What d'you mean by 'know'?" As that was a difficult question to answer off-hand, I passed it over by saying: "Well, at any rate they'll be able to make their livings and teach other people." Whereupon she lost her temper and, seizing the unfortunate work upon the Elizabethan sonnet, whizzed it across the room. The rest of the visit passed in picking up the fragments of a teapot that had belonged to her grandmother.

Now of course a dozen other questions clamour to be asked about churches and parliaments and public houses and shops and loudspeakers and men and women; but mercifully time is up; silence falls.

PROFESSIONS FOR WOMEN
(* A paper read to The Women's Service League.)

When your secretary invited me to come here, she told me that your Society is concerned with the employment of women and she suggested that I might tell you something about my own professional experiences. It is true I am a woman; it is true I am employed; but what professional experiences have I had? It is difficult to say. My profession is literature; and in that profession there are fewer experiences for women than in any other, with the exception of the stage--fewer, I mean, that are peculiar to women. For the road was cut many years ago--by Fanny Burney, by Aphra Behn, by Harriet Martineau, by Jane Austen, by George Eliot--many famous women, and many more unknown and forgotten, have been before me, making the path smooth, and regulating my steps. Thus, when I came to write, there were very few material obstacles in my way. Writing was a reputable and harmless occupation. The family peace was not broken by the scratching of a pen. No demand was made upon the family purse. For ten and sixpence one can buy paper enough to write all the plays of Shakespeare--if one has a mind that way. Pianos and models, Paris, Vienna and Berlin, masters and mistresses, are not needed by a writer. The cheapness of writing paper is, of course, the reason why women have succeeded as writers before they have succeeded in the other professions.

But to tell you my story--it is a simple one. You have only

got to figure to yourselves a girl in a bedroom with a pen in her hand. She had only to move that pen from left to right--from ten o'clock to one. Then it occurred to her to do what is simple and cheap enough after all--to slip a few of those pages into an envelope, fix a penny stamp in the corner, and drop the envelope into the red box at the corner. It was thus that I became a journalist; and my effort was rewarded on the first day of the following month--a very glorious day it was for me--by a letter from an editor containing a cheque for one pound ten shillings and sixpence. But to show you how little I deserve to be called a professional woman, how little I know of the struggles and difficulties of such lives, I have to admit that instead of spending that sum upon bread and butter, rent, shoes and stockings, or butcher's bills, I went out and bought a cat--a beautiful cat, a Persian cat, which very soon involved me in bitter disputes with my neighbours.

What could be easier than to write articles and to buy Persian cats with the profits? But wait a moment. Articles have to be about something. Mine, I seem to remember, was about a novel by a famous man. And while I was writing this review, I discovered that if I were going to review books I should need to do battle with a certain phantom. And the phantom was a woman, and when I came to know her better I called her after the heroine of a famous poem, The Angel in the House. It was she who used to come between me and my paper when I was writing reviews. It was she who bothered me and wasted my time and so tormented me that at last I killed her. You who come of a younger and happier generation may not have heard of her--you may not know what I mean by the Angel in the House. I will describe her as shortly as I can. She was intensely sympathetic. She was immensely charming. She was utterly unselfish. She excelled in the difficult arts of family life. She sacrificed herself daily. If there was chicken, she took the leg; if there was a draught she sat in it--in short she was so constituted that she never had a mind or a wish of her own, but preferred to sympathize always with the minds and wishes of others. Above all--I need not say it---she was pure. Her purity was supposed to be her chief beauty--her blushes, her great grace. In those days--the last of Queen Victoria--every house had its Angel. And when I came to write I encountered her with the very first words. The shadow of her wings fell on my page; I heard the rustling of her skirts in the room. Directly, that is to say, I took my pen in my hand to review that novel by a famous man, she slipped behind me and whispered: "My dear, you are a young woman. You are writing about a book that has been written by a man. Be sympathetic; be tender; flatter; deceive; use all the arts and wiles of our sex. Never let anybody guess that you have a mind of your own. Above all, be pure." And she made as if to guide my pen. I now record the one act for which I take some credit to myself, though the credit rightly belongs to some excellent ancestors of mine who left me a certain sum of money--shall we say five hundred pounds a year?--so that it was not necessary for me to depend solely on charm for my living. I turned upon her and caught her by the throat. I did my best to kill her. My excuse, if I were to be had up in a court of law, would be that I acted in self-defence. Had I not killed her she would have killed me. She would have plucked the heart out of my writing. For, as I found, directly I put pen to paper, you cannot review even a novel without having a mind of your own, without expressing what you think to be the truth about human relations, morality, sex. And all these questions, according to the Angel of the House, cannot be dealt with freely and openly by women; they must charm, they must conciliate, they must--to put it bluntly--tell lies if they are to succeed. Thus, whenever I felt the shadow of her wing or the radiance of her halo upon my page, I took up the inkpot and flung it at her. She died hard. Her fictitious nature was of great assistance to her. It is far harder to kill a phantom than a reality. She was always creeping back when I thought I had despatched her. Though I flatter myself that I killed her in the end, the struggle was severe; it took much time that had better have been spent upon learning Greek grammar; or in roaming the world in search of adventures. But it was a real experience; it was an experience that was bound to befall all women writers at that time. Killing the Angel in the House was part of the occupation of a woman writer.

But to continue my story. The Angel was dead; what then remained? You may say that what remained was a simple and common object--a young woman in a bedroom with an inkpot. In other words, now that she had rid herself of falsehood, that young woman had only to be herself. Ah, but what is "herself"? I mean, what is a woman? I assure you, I do not know. I do not believe that you know. I do not believe that anybody can know until she has expressed herself in all the arts and professions open to human skill. That indeed is one of the reasons why I have come here out of respect for you, who are in process of showing us by your experiments what a woman is, who are in process Of providing us, by your failures and successes, with that extremely important piece of information.

But to continue the story of my professional experiences. I made one pound ten and six by my first review; and I bought a Persian cat with the proceeds. Then I grew ambitious. A Persian cat is all very well, I said; but a Persian cat is not enough. I must have a motor car. And it was thus that I became a novelist--for it is a very strange thing that people will give you a motor car if you will tell them a story. It is a still stranger thing that there is nothing so delightful in the world as telling stories. It is far pleasanter than writing reviews of famous novels. And yet, if I am to obey your secretary and tell you my professional experiences as a novelist, I must tell you about a very strange experience that befell me as a novelist. And to understand it you must try first to imagine a novelist's state of mind. I hope I am not giving away professional secrets if I say that a novelist's chief desire is to be as unconscious as possible. He has to induce in himself a state of perpetual lethargy. He wants life to proceed with the utmost quiet and regularity. He wants to see the same faces, to read the same books, to do the same things day after day, month after month, while he is writing, so that nothing may break the illusion in which he is living--so that nothing may disturb or disquiet the mysterious nosings about, feelings round, darts, dashes and sudden discoveries of that very shy and illusive spirit, the imagination. I suspect that this state is the same both for men and women. Be that as it may, I want you to imagine me writing a novel in a state of trance. I want you to figure to yourselves a girl sitting with a pen in her hand, which for minutes, and indeed for hours, she never dips into the inkpot. The image that comes to my mind when I think of this girl is the image of a fisherman lying sunk in dreams on the verge of a deep lake with a rod held out over the water. She was letting her imagination sweep unchecked round every rock and cranny of the world that lies submerged in the depths of our unconscious being. Now came the experience, the experience that I believe to be far commoner with women writers than with men. The line raced through the girl's fingers. Her imagination had rushed away. It had sought the pools, the depths, the dark places where the largest fish slumber. And then there was a smash. There was an explosion. There was foam and confusion. The imagination had dashed itself against something hard. The girl was roused from her dream. She was indeed in a state of the most acute and difficult distress. To speak without figure she had thought of something, something about the body, about the passions which it was unfitting for her as a woman to say. Men, her reason told her, would be shocked. The consciousness of--what men will say of a woman who speaks the truth about her passions had roused her from her artist's state of unconsciousness. She could write no more. The trance was over. Her imagination could work no longer. This I believe to be a very common experience with women writers--they are impeded by the extreme conventionality of the other sex. For though men sensibly allow themselves great freedom in these respects, I doubt that they realize or can control the extreme severity with which they condemn such freedom in women.

These then were two very genuine experiences of my own. These were two of the adventures of my professional life. The first--killing the Angel in the House--I think I solved. She died. But the second, telling the truth about my own experiences as a body, I do not think I solved. I doubt that any woman has solved it yet. The obstacles against her are still immensely powerful--and yet they are very difficult to define. Outwardly, what is simpler than to write books? Outwardly, what obstacles are there for a woman rather than for a man? Inwardly, I think, the case is very different; she has still many ghosts to fight, many prejudices to overcome. Indeed it will be a long time still, I think, before a woman can sit down to write a book without finding a phantom to be slain, a rock to be dashed against. And if this is so in literature, the freest of all professions for women, how is it in the new professions which you are now for the first time entering?

Those are the questions that I should like, had I time, to ask you. And indeed, if I have laid stress upon these professional experiences of mine, it is because I believe that they are, though in different forms, yours also. Even when the path is nominally open--when there is nothing to prevent a woman from being a doctor, a lawyer, a civil servant--there are many phantoms and obstacles, as I believe, looming in her way. To discuss and define them is I think of great value and importance; for thus only can the labour be shared, the difficulties be solved. But besides this, it is necessary also to discuss the ends and the aims for which we are fighting, for which we are doing battle with these formidable obstacles. Those aims cannot be taken for granted; they must be perpetually questioned and examined. The whole position, as I see it--here in this hall surrounded by women practising for the first time in history I know not how many different professions--is one of extraordinary interest and importance. You have won rooms of your own in the house hitherto exclusively owned by men. You are able, though not without great labour and effort, to pay the rent. You are earning your five hundred pounds a year. But this freedom is only a beginning--the room is your own, but it is still bare. It has to be furnished; it has to be decorated; it has to be shared. How are you going to furnish it, how are you going to decorate it? With whom are you going to share it, and upon what terms? These, I think are questions of the utmost importance and interest. For the first time in history you are able to ask them; for the first time you are able to decide for yourselves what the answers should be. Willingly would I stay and discuss those questions and answers--but not to-night. My time is up; and I must cease.

THOUGHTS ON PEACE IN AN AIR RAID
(* Written in August 1940, for an American symposium on current matters concerning women.)

The Germans were over this house last night and the night before that. Here they are again. It is a queer experience, lying in the dark and listening to the zoom of a hornet which may at any moment sting you to death. It is a sound that interrupts cool and consecutive thinking about peace. Yet it is a sound--far more than prayers and anthems--that should compel one to think about peace. Unless we can think peace into existence we---not this one body in this one bed but millions of bodies yet to be born--will lie in the same darkness and hear the same death rattle overhead. Let us think what we can do to create the only efficient air-raid shelter while the guns on the hill go pop pop pop and the searchlights finger the clouds and now and then, sometimes close at hand, sometimes far away, a bomb drops.

Up there in the sky young Englishmen and young German men are fighting each other. The defenders are men, the attackers are men. Arms are not given to Englishwomen either to fight the enemy or to defend herself. She must lie weaponless to-night. Yet if she believes that the fight going on up in the sky is a fight by the English to protect freedom, by the Germans to destroy freedom, she must fight, so far as she can, on the side of the English. How far can she fight for freedom without firearms? By making arms, or clothes or food. But there is another way of fighting for freedom without arms; we can fight with the mind. We can make ideas that will help the young Englishman who is fighting up in the sky to defeat the enemy.

But to make ideas effective, we must be able to fire them off. We must put them into action. And the hornet in the sky rouses another hornet in the mind. There was one zooming in THE TIMES this morning--a woman's voice saying, "Women have not a word to say in politics." There is no woman in the Cabinet; nor in any responsible post. All the idea makers who are in a position to make ideas effective are men. That is a thought that damps thinking, and encourages irresponsibility. Why not bury the head in the pillow, plug the ears, and cease this futile activity of idea-making? Because there are other tables besides officer tables and conference tables. Are we not leaving the young Englishman without a weapon that might be of value to him if we give up private thinking, tea-table thinking, because it seems useless? Are we not stressing our disability because our ability exposes us perhaps to abuse, perhaps to contempt? "I will not cease from mental fight," Blake wrote. Mental fight means thinking against the current, not with it.

That current flows fast and furious. It issues in a spate of words from the loudspeakers and the politicians. Every day they tell us that we are a free people, fighting to defend freedom. That is the current that has whirled the young airman up into the sky and keeps him circling there among the clouds. Down here, with a roof to cover us and a gas mask handy, it is our business to puncture gas bags and discover seeds of truth. It is not true that we are free. We are both prisoners to-night--he boxed up in his machine with a gun handy; we lying in the dark with a gas mask handy. If we were free we should be out in the open, dancing, at the play, or sitting at the window talking together. What is it that prevents us? "Hitler!" the loudspeakers cry with one voice. Who is Hitler? What is he? Aggressiveness, tyranny, the insane love of power made manifest, they reply. Destroy that, and you will be free.

The drone of the planes is now like the sawing of a branch overhead. Round and round it goes, sawing and sawing at a branch directly above the house. Another sound begins sawing its way in the brain. "Women of ability"--it was Lady Astor speaking in THE TIMES this morning--"are held down because of a subconscious Hitlerism in the hearts of men." Certainly we are held down. We are equally prisoners tonight--the Englishmen in their planes, the Englishwomen in their beds. But if he stops to think he may be killed; and we too. So let us think for him. Let us try to drag up into consciousness the subconscious Hitlerism that holds us down. It is the desire for aggression; the desire to dominate and enslave. Even in the darkness we can see that made visible. We can see shop windows blazing; and women gazing; painted women; dressed-up women; women with crimson lips and crimson fingernails. They are slaves who are trying to enslave. If we could free ourselves from slavery we should free men from tyranny. Hitlers are bred by slaves.

A bomb drops. All the windows rattle. The anti-aircraft

guns are getting active. Up there on the hill under a net tagged with strips of green and brown stuff to imitate the hues of autumn leaves, guns are concealed. Now they all fire at once. On the nine o'clock radio we shall be told "Forty-four enemy planes were shot down during the night, ten of them by anti-aircraft fire." And one of the terms of peace, the loudspeakers say, is to be disarmament. There are to be no more guns, no army, no navy, no air force in the future. No more young men will be trained to fight with arms. That rouses another mind-hornet in the chambers of the brain--another quotation. "To fight against a real enemy, to earn undying honour and glory by shooting total strangers, and to come home with my breast covered with medals and decorations, that was the summit of my hope.... It was for this that my whole life so far had been dedicated, my education, training, everything...."

Those were the words of a young Englishman who fought in the last war. In the face of them, do the current thinkers honestly believe that by writing "Disarmament" on a sheet of paper at a conference table they will have done all that is needful? Othello's occupation will be gone; but he will remain Othello. The young airman up in the sky is driven not only by the voices of loudspeakers; he is driven by voices in himself--ancient instincts, instincts fostered and cherished by education and tradition. Is he to be blamed for those instincts? Could we switch off the maternal instinct at the command of a table full of politicians? Suppose that imperative among the peace terms was: "Child-bearing is to be restricted to a very small class of specially selected women," would we submit? Should we not say, "The maternal instinct is a woman's glory. It was for this that my whole life has been dedicated, my education, training, everything. . . ." But if it were necessary. for the sake of humanity, for the peace of the world, that childbearing should be restricted, the maternal instinct subdued, women would attempt it. Men would help them. They would honour them for their refusal to bear children. They would give them other openings for their creative power. That too must make part of our fight for freedom. We must help the young Englishmen to root out from themselves the love of medals and decorations. We must create more honourable activities for those who try to conquer in themselves their fighting instinct, their subconscious Hitlerism. We must compensate the man for the loss of his gun.

The sound of sawing overhead has increased. All the searchlights are erect. They point at a spot exactly above this roof. At any moment a bomb may fall on this very room. One, two, three, four, five, six . . . the seconds pass. The bomb did not fall. But during those seconds of suspense all thinking stopped. All feeling, save one dull dread, ceased. A nail fixed the whole being to one hard board. The emotion of fear and of hate is therefore sterile, unfertile. Directly that fear passes, the mind reaches out and instinctively revives itself by trying to create. Since the room is dark it can create only from memory. It reaches out to the memory of other Augusts--in Bayreuth, listening to Wagner; in Rome, walking over the Campagna; in London. Friends' voices come back. Scraps of poetry return. Each of those thoughts, even in memory, was far more positive, reviving, healing and creative than the dull dread made of fear and hate. Therefore if we are to compensate the young man for the loss of his glory and of his gun, we must give him access to the creative feelings. We must make happiness. We must free him from the machine. We must bring him out of his prison into the open air. But what is the use of freeing the young Englishman if the young German and the young Italian remain slaves?

The searchlights, wavering across the flat, have picked up the plane now. From this window one can see a little silver insect turning and twisting in the light. The guns go pop pop pop. Then they cease. Probably the raider was brought down behind the hill. One of the pilots landed safe in a field near here the other day. He said to his captors, speaking fairly good English, "How glad I am that the fight is over!" Then an Englishman gave him a cigarette, and an Englishwoman made him a cup of tea. That would seem to show that if you can free the man from the machine, the seed does not fall upon altogether stony ground. The seed may be fertile.

At last all the guns have stopped firing. All the searchlights have been extinguished. The natural darkness of a summer's night returns. The innocent sounds of the country are heard again. An apple thuds to the ground. An owl hoots, winging its way from tree to tree. And some half-forgotten words of an old English writer come to mind: "The huntsmen are up in America. . . ." Let us send these fragmentary notes to the huntsmen who are up in America, to the men and women whose sleep has not yet been broken by machine-gun fire, in the belief that they will rethink them generously and charitably, perhaps shape them into something serviceable. And now, in the shadowed half of the world, to sleep.

THE END

Lightning Source UK Ltd.
Milton Keynes UK
UKHW040629170122
397276UK00001B/89